"Looking back over the years, they have been wonderful and heartbreaking, frustrating and joyous — all rolled into one. We have been two people constantly learning to blend our personalities and wills into that mystical union — marriage. ... The prayer we pray for ourselves, we pray for you to be brought closer together each day."

Together Each Day brings into sharp focus the unique relationship God intends for those He has joined as one flesh — and what each of you can do to make that fulfillment an everyday reality. Joan Winmill Brown and her husband, Bill, draw upon a wealth of Scripture, Christian sources, and the sensitivity and insight gained through their own lifelong commitment to one another — and to the Lord. Now you can enjoy deeper fellowship together as you learn how to nurture your oneness in Christ by sharing devotions *Together Each Day*.

BY Joan Winmill Brown

No Longer Alone
Day by Day With Billy Graham
Wings of Joy
Every Knee Shall Bow
Corrie: The Lives She's Touched

BY Joan Winmill Brown and Bill Brown

Together Each Day

TOGETHER EACH DAY

Joan Winmill Brown and Bill Brown

Power Books

Fleming H. Revell Company
Old Tappan, New Jersey

Library of Congress Cataloging in Publication Data

Main entry under title:

Together each day.

    Includes index.
    1. Devotional calendars. I. Brown, Joan Winmill.
II. Brown, Bill, 1927–
BV4810.T64   242′.2   80–20539
ISBN 0–8007 5226–0

TO
Bill, Jr., and Donna

Contents

Acknowledgments

Acknowledgment is made to the following for permission to reprint copyrighted material:

ACCENT BOOKS: excerpts from *Your Marriage Needs Three Love Affairs,* by John Allan Lavender. Accent Books, Denver, Colorado, 1978. Used by permission.

AFRICAN ENTERPRISE: excerpts from *The Spirit Is Moving,* by Festo Kivengere, African Enterprise, Pasadena, CA, 1979

ARGUS COMMUNICATIONS: excerpts from *He Touched Me,* by John Powell, S. J., © 1974 Argus Communications, Niles, IL. Excerpts from *Why Am I Afraid to Love?* by John Powell, S.J., © 1967 Argus Communications, Niles, IL.

AUGSBURG PUBLISHING HOUSE: excerpts from *The Friendship Factor,* by Alan Loy McGinnis, copyright 1979, used by permission of Augsburg Publishing House.

BAKER BOOK HOUSE: excerpts from *God's Plan for Your Marriage*, by Tim Timmons, Copyright 1974 by Baker Book House and used by permission.

BETHANY FELLOWSHIP, INC.: excerpts from THE CHRISTIAN FAMILY by Larry Christenson, published and copyright 1970. Bethany Fellowship, Inc., Minneapolis, MN 55438.

BIBLE VOICE, INC.: excerpts from *Pat Boone Devotional Book,* by Pat Boone with Dan O'Neill, © 1977. Excerpts from *To Adam With Love,* by Douglas Roberts, copyright 1974 Bible Voice Publishers.

THE BILLY GRAHAM EVANGELISTIC ASSOCIATION: excerpts from DECISION by Leighton Ford © 1969 by The Billy Graham Evangelistic Association. Excerpts from *Day by Day With Billy Graham,* © 1969 by the Billy Graham Evangelistic Association, used by permission. Excerpts from *Great Reading From Decision,* © 1960 by the Billy Graham Evangelistic Association, used by permission.

BROADMAN PRESS: excerpts from *Finding God's Best,* by John Hunter (Nashville: Broadman Press, 1975). All rights reserved. Used by permission.

CHOSEN BOOKS: excerpts from *Something More* © 1974 by Catherine Marshall LeSourd. Published by Chosen Books, Lincoln, VA 22078. Used by permission. *Adventures In Prayer* © 1975 by Catherine Marshall; published by Chosen Books, Lincoln, Va. 22078. Used by permission. *To Live Again* © by Catherine Marshall. Published by Chosen Books, Lincoln, VA 22078. Used by permission.

WILLIAM COLLINS SONS & CO.: excerpts from *Mere Christianity* by C. S. Lewis used by permission of William Collins Sons & Co., Ltd.

DOUBLEDAY & COMPANY, INC.: excerpts from *The Life of Christ*, by Fulton J. Sheen copyright © 1958, 1977 by Fulton J. Sheen. Reprinted by permission of Doubleday & Company, Inc. Excerpts from *Talk To Me* by Charlie W. Shedd. Copyright ©1975 by Charlie W. Shedd and The Abundance Foundation. Reprinted by permission of Doubleday and Company, Inc. Excerpt and "Psalm For Marriage" from *I've Got to Talk to Somebody, God* by Marjorie Holmes. Copyright © 1968, 1969 by Marjorie Holmes Mighell. Reprinted by permission of Doubleday and Company, Inc. Excerpts from *Jesus Rediscovered* by Malcolm Muggeridge. Copyright © 1969 by Malcolm Muggeridge. Reprinted by permission of Doubleday and Company, Inc. Excerpts from *The Guideposts Treasury of Love* © 1978 by Guideposts Associates. Used by permission of Doubleday and Company, Inc.

WILLIAM B. EERDMANS PUBLISHING CO.: excerpts from *Convictions to Live By*, by L. Nelson Bell (Grand Rapids, Wm. B. Eerdmans Publishing Company, 1966). Excerpts from *Love Within Limits*, by Lewis B. Smedes (Grand Rapids, Wm. B. Eerdmans Publishing Co. 1978).

GOSPEL LIGHT PUBLICATIONS: excerpts reprinted from *Let's Get Moving* (Regal book) by D. Stuart Briscoe. © Copyright 1978 Gospel Light Publications, Glendale, CA 91209. Used by permission. Excerpts from *Love Unlimited* (Regal book) by Bishop Festo Kivengere, © Copyright 1975 G/L Publications, Glendale, CA 91209. Used by permission. Excerpts from *421 Quotes* (Regal book), by Dr. Henrietta C. Mears, © Copyright 1970 Gospel Light Publications, Glendale, CA 91209. Used by permission. Excerpts from *Sex Is A Parent Affair* (Regal book), by Letha Scanzoni, © Copyright 1973 Gospel Light Publications, Glendale, CA 91209. Used by permission.

HARPER & ROW: "Let Us Keep Christmas" from *Poems of Inspiration and Courage,* by Grace Noll Crowell, copyright 1950 by Harper & Row, Publishers, Inc. Reprinted by permission of the publisher. Excerpts from pages 69, 72 *SOMETHING BEAUTIFUL FOR GOD* by Malcolm Muggeridge. Copyright © 1971 by The Mother Teresa Committee. Reprinted by Permission of Harper & Row, Publishers, Inc. Excerpt from page 45 of *LOVE IS SOMETHING YOU DO,* by John R. Bisagno. Copyright © 1975 by John R. Bisagno. Reprinted by permission of Harper & Row, Publishers, Inc. Excerpt from pages 4, 49, 80, *I LOVED A GIRL* by Walter Trobisch. Copyright © 1963, 1964 by Walter Trobisch. Reprinted by permission of Harper & Row, Publishers, Inc. Excerpts from pages 138, 165, 176, 167–68 in *THE MEANING OF PERSONS* by Paul Tournier. Copyright © 1957 by Paul Tournier. Reprinted by permission of Harper & Row, Publishers, Inc.

HARVEST HOUSE PUBLISHERS: excerpt from *Put Love In Your Marriage,* by Lou Beardsley, Copyright 1975, Harvest House Publishers, Irvine, CA 92714. Excerpts from *The Art Of Married Love,* by Pamela Heim, Copyright 1979, Harvest House Publishers, Irvine, CA 92714. Excerpts from *Living Without Losing,* by Don H. Polston, Copyright 1978, Harvest House Publishers, Irvine, CA 92714. Excerpts from *Daily Power Thoughts,* by Robert H. Schuller, copyright Robert Schuller. Published by Harvest House Publishers, Irvine, CA 92714.

HERALD PRESS: excerpts from *When You Don't Agree,* by James G. T. Fairfield (Scottdale, PA: Herald Press, 1977) used by permission.

HODDER & STOUGHTON, LTD: excerpts from *Walk in His Steps,* by John R. W. Stott, © 1967 by Evangelical Fellowship in the Anglican Communion.

INTER-VARSITY PRESS: excerpts from *Walk In His Shoes,* by John R. W. Stott, by permission of Inter-Varsity Press. Leicester, Great Britain, © 1975.

KEATS PUBLISHING: excerpts from *Daily Strength for Daily Needs,* by Mary W. Tileston, edition published by Keats Publishing, Inc., New Canaan, CT. Special contents © by Keats Publishing, Inc.

CATHERINE MARSHALL LE SOURD: excerpts from *Mr. Jones, Meet the Master,* © Catherine Marshall 1954.

MOODY PRESS: excerpts from *Toward a Growing Marriage,* by Gary Chapman, copyright 1979, Moody Press, Moody Bible Institute of Chicago. Used by permission.

MULTNOMAH PRESS: excerpt from the book *Home: Where Life Makes Up Its Mind* by Charles R. Swindoll, © 1979 by Multnomah Press, Portland, Oregon 97266. Used by permission. Excerpt from the book *For Those Who Hurt,* by Chuck Swindoll, © 1977 by Multnomah Press, Portland, Oregon 97266. Used by permission.

NAVPRESS: excerpts from *Marriage Takes More Than Love,* by Jack and Carole Mayhall, © 1978 by The Navigators. Published by NavPress, Colorado Springs, Colorado. Used by permission. All rights reserved.

PAULIST PRESS: excerpts from *To Give the Love of Christ,* by James McGovern, © 1978 by The Missionary Society of St. Paul the Apostle in the State of New York. Used by permission of Paulist Press.

FLEMING H. REVELL CO.: excerpts from "The Touch of Faith" in *Mr. Jones, Meet the Master:* Sermons and Prayers of Peter Marshall. Edited by Catherine Marshall. Copyright © 1949, 1959 by Fleming H. Revell Company. Renewed 1976, 1977 by Catherine Marshall Le Sourd. Used by permission. Excerpts from *What Is a Family?* by Edith Schaeffer, copyright © 1975 by Edith Schaeffer. Published by Fleming H. Revell Company. Used by permission. Excerpts from *A Tramp Finds a Home,* by Corrie ten Boom, copyright © 1978 by Corrie ten Boom. Published by Fleming H. Revell Co. Used by permission. Excerpt from *They Call Me Mother Graham,* by Morrow C. Graham, copyright © 1977 by Fleming H. Revell Co. Used by permission. Excerpts from *Established in Eden,* by Carole C. Carlson, copyright © 1978 by Carole C. Carlson. Published by Fleming H. Revell Co. Used by permission. Excerpts from *Perfect Peace,* by Charles L. Allen, copyright © 1979 by Charles L.

Allen. Published by Fleming H. Revell Co. Used by permission. Excerpt from *Love Is an Everyday Thing* by Colleen Townsend Evans, copyright © 1974 by Fleming H. Revell Co. Used by permission. Excerpts from *My Lover, My Friend,* by Colleen Townsend Evans and Louis H. Evans, Jr., copyright © 1976 by Fleming H. Revell Co. Used by permission. Excerpts from *Some Run With Feet of Clay,* by Jeannette Clift, copyright © 1978 by Jeannette Clift George. Published by Fleming H. Revell Co. Used by permission. Excerpts from *LUST:* The Other Side of Love, by Mel White, copyright © 1978 by Mel White. Published by Fleming H. Revell Co. Used by permission. Excerpts from *Let's Live!* by C. C. Mitchell, copyright © 1975 by Fleming H. Revell Co. Used by permission. Excerpts from *Tramp for the Lord,* by Corrie ten Boom with Jamie Buckingham, copyright © 1974 by Corrie ten Boom and Jamie Buckingham. Published cooperatively by Christian Literature Crusade and Fleming H. Revell Co. Used by permission. Excerpt from *Don't Wrestle, Just Nestle,* by Corrie ten Boom, copyright © 1978 by Corrie ten Boom. Published by Fleming H. Revell Co. Used by permission. Excerpts from *Victorious Praying,* by Alan Redpath, copyright © 1957 by Fleming H. Revell Co. Used by permission. Excerpts from *Law and Liberty,* by Alan Redpath, copyright © 1978 by Allan Redpath. Published by Fleming H. Revell Co. Used by permission. Excerpts from *For Such a Time as This,* by Vonette Zachary Bright, copyright © 1976 by Fleming H. Revell Co. Used by permission. Excerpts from *To Pray Is to Live,* by William P. Barker, copyright © 1977 by Fleming H. Revell Co. Used by permission. Excerpts from *Every Knee Shall Bow,* by Joan Winmill Brown, copyright © 1978 by Joan Winmill Brown. Published by Fleming H. Revell Co. Used by permission. Excerpt from *Power Ideas for a Happy Family,* by Robert H. Schuller, copyright © 1972 by Robert Harold Schuller. Published by Fleming H. Revell Co. Used by permission. Excerpts from *My Prayer for You,* by Pat Robertson, copyright © 1977 by M. G. Robertson. Published by Fleming H. Revell Co. Used by permission. Excerpts from *Christmas,* by Charles L. Allen and Charles L. Wallis, copyright © 1957, 1959, 1963, 1977 by Fleming H. Revell Co. Used by permission. Excerpts from *Victorious Christian Living,* by Alan Redpath, copyright © 1955 by Fleming H. Revell Co. Used by permission. Excerpt from *Victorious Christian Service,* by Alan Redpath, copyright © 1958 by Fleming H. Revell Co. Used by permission. Excerpt from *Truths That Transform,* by D. James Kennedy, copyright © 1974 by D. James Kennedy. Published by Fleming H. Revell Co. Used by permission. Excerpt from *The Woman At the Well,* by Dale Evans Rogers, copyright © 1970 by Fleming H. Revell Co. Used by permission. Excerpts from *After You've Said I Do,* by Dwight Hervey Small, copyright © 1968 by Fleming H. Revell Co. Used by permission. Excerpts from *Your Marriage Is God's Affair,* by Dwight Hervey Small, copyright © 1979 by Dwight Hervey Small. Published by Fleming H. Revell Co. Used by permission. Excerpt from *Power for Living,* by Daniel C. Steere, copyright © 1977 by Daniel C. Steere. Published by Fleming H. Revell Co. Used by permission. Excerpts from *Time Out, Ladies!* by Dale Evans Rogers, copyright © 1966 by Fleming H. Revell Co. Used by permission. Excerpt from *Husband-Wife Equality,* by Herbert J. Miles and Fern Harrington Miles, copyright © 1978 by Herbert J. Miles and Fern Harrington Miles. Published by Fleming H. Revell Co. Used by permission. Excerpts from *Dark Threads the Weaver Needs,* by Herbert Lockyer, copyright © 1979 by Herbert Lockyer. Published by Fleming H. Revell Co. Used by permission. Excerpts from *Tough and Tender,* by Joyce Landorf, copyright © 1975 by Fleming H. Revell Co. Used by permission. Excerpts from

Spirit Controlled Family Living by Tim and Bev LaHaye, copyright © 1978 by Tim and Bev LaHaye. Published by Fleming H. Revell Co. Used by permission. Excerpts from *The Christian's Secret of a Happy Life for Today,* by Catherine Jackson, copyright © 1979 by Catherine Jackson. Published by Fleming H. Revell Co. Used by permission. Excerpts from *The People You Live With,* by O. Quentin Hyder, M. D., copyright © 1975 by Fleming H. Revell Co. Used by permission. Excerpts from *Feeling Free,* by Archibald D. Hart, copyright © 1979 by Archibald D. Hart. Published by Fleming H. Revell Co. Used by permission. Excerpts from *Because He Lives,* by Gloria Gaither, copyright © 1977 by Gloria Gaither. Published by Fleming H. Revell Co. Used by permission. Excerpt from *The Miracle of Love,* by Charles L. Allen, copyright © 1972 by Fleming H. Revell Co. Used by permission. Excerpts from *Affliction,* by Edith Schaeffer, copyright © 1978 by Edith Schaeffer. Published by Fleming H. Revell Co. Used by permission.

SEABURY PRESS: excerpts from *A Grief Observed,* by C. S. Lewis, copyright © 1961 by N. W. Clerk. Used by permission of the Seabury Press Inc.

HAROLD SHAW PUBLISHERS: excerpts from *Faith Under Fire,* by David Winter, reprinted by permission of Harold Shaw Publishers. Copyright © 1977 by Harold Shaw Publishers.

TYNDALE HOUSE PUBLISHERS, INC.: excerpts from *The Joyful Heart,* by Watchman Nee. Excerpts from *Roads A Christian Must Travel,* by Merrill C. Tenney, published by Tyndale House Publishers, Inc., © 1979. Used by permission. Excerpts from *Magnificent Marriage,* by Gordon MacDonald, published by Tyndale House Publishers, Inc., © 1976. Used by permission. Excerpts from *How Come It's Taking Me So Long To Get Better?* by Lane Adams, published by Tyndale House Publishers, Inc., © 1975 by Lane Adams. Used by permission. Excerpts from *Let Me Be A Woman,* by Elisabeth Elliot, published by Tyndale House Publishers, Inc., © 1976. Used by permission. Excerpts from *What Wives Wish Their Husbands Knew About Women,* by Dr. James Dobson, published by Tyndale House Publishers, Inc., © 1975. Used by permission. Excerpts from *7 Keys to Maximum Communication,* by Dr. Paul Cedar, published by Tyndale House Publishers, Inc., © 1980 by Dr. Paul Cedar. Used by permission. Excerpts from *Cup of Wonder,* by Lloyd John Ogilvie, published by Tyndale House Publishers, Inc., © 1976. Used by permission.

VICTOR BOOKS; excerpts from *Two to Get Ready,* © 1978 by Anthony Florio, used by permission of Victor Books.

VISION HOUSE PUBLISHERS: excerpts from *Characteristics of a Caring Home,* by H. Norman Wright and Rex Johnson, copyright © 1978 Vision House Publishers, Santa Ana, CA 92705. All rights reserved.

WESTMINSTER PRESS: excerpts from *Whom God Hath Joined* (Revised Edition), by David R. Mace, © The Epworth Press 1953, 1973. Used by permission of the Westminster Press.

WORD BOOKS: excerpts from *Life Without Limits,* by Lloyd John Ogilvie. Excerpts from *Happy Trails,* by Roy Rogers and Dale Evans. Excerpts from *A Gardener Looks at the Fruits of the Spirit,* by W. Phillip Keller. Excerpts from *Is There a Family in the House?* by Kenneth Chafin.

Poetry by Ruth Bell Graham from *Sitting by my Laughing Fire* copyright © 1977 by Ruth Bell Graham.

ZONDERVAN PUBLISHING HOUSE: excerpts from *The Fullness of Christ,* by D. Stuart Briscoe. Copyright © 1965 by Zondervan Publishing House. Excerpts from *Hush, Hush!* by Jill Briscoe. Copyright © 1978 by The Zondervan Corporation. Excerpts from *A Step Further,* by Joni Eareckson and Steve Estes. Copyright © 1978 by Joni Eareckson & Steve Estes. Used by permission of Zondervan Publishing House. Excerpts from *A Shepherd Looks at Psalm 23,* by W. Phillip Keller. Copyright © 1970 by W. Phillip Keller. Used by permission of Zondervan Publishing House. Excerpt from *The Richest Lady in Town,* by Joyce Landorf, Copyright © 1973 by The Zondervan Corporation. Excerpts from *To Live in Love,* by Eileen Guder, copyright © 1967 by Zondervan Publishing House. Used by permission.

Introduction

During the time Bill and I gathered and wrote the material for this devotional, we celebrated our twenty-fifth wedding anniversary. Looking back over the years, they have been wonderful and heartbreaking, frustrating and joyous—all rolled into one. We have been two people *constantly* learning to blend our personalities and wills into that mystical union—marriage.

We were exact opposites, from different countries (Bill from America, and I from England), different cultures. It seemed everything had to be relearned, especially thinking of the other's needs, as well as our own.

I remember, just after a few weeks of marriage, I said to Bill, "You know, without the Lord, we would never be able to make it!" He looked at me incredulously and said, "Surely it hasn't been *that* bad, has it?"

But we had one common denominator: our faith in Jesus Christ. Knowing He understood our weaknesses and still loved us has, through the years, healed hurts, settled arguments, and given us a deeper love for each other. Quite frankly, *we* think honeymoons are overrated, compared to the thrill and excitement of a silver wedding celebration!

Also during the time we were compiling this book, our oldest son, Bill, Jr., was married. Throughout the twenty-three years of his life we had prayed for the girl he would marry, and God brought into his life a beautiful, sensitive, loving Christian—Donna. Our hearts were filled with thankfulness to our Lord. On their wedding day, Bill and I sat together in the church, holding hands, remembering *our* wedding day. Memories raced through my mind: the adjustments, the hurdles that had to be faced when we left the beauty of our ceremony, where we had sincerely repeated vows "for better or for worse," and had to begin the reality of the everyday routine of living together.

Every mother wants to shield her children from life's hurts, but it is only in living through them that children can learn. That day, at my son's wedding, I wished I could shield Bill and Donna from all the hurts that would cross their paths in years to come, but I knew I could not. Then, too, I wished I could convey the full beauty of those many times when the joy of marriage would be uniquely shared.

As Bill, Sr., and I have had to learn by experience, so will they: By putting Jesus Christ first, He supplies the grace and love needed for every situation.

This book is lovingly written and compiled for all those of you who are married. May it be a source of enrichment during your years together, deepening your love for each other and for our Lord Jesus Christ.

We have brought together the writings of others whose words have been a comfort and blessing to us. Bill and I thank them for the positive and joyous influence their words have been in our lives and for granting us permission to share their works with you.

Spending time together with the Lord has protected our home and relationship. The prayer we pray for ourselves, we pray for you: to be brought closer *together each day.*

JOAN WINMILL BROWN

Love is longsuffering
and kind;
love is not jealous,
or boastful or arrogant or rude.
Love does not seek its own;
it is not irritable
or resentful;
it does not rejoice in evil,
but rejoices with the truth.
Love bears all things,
believes all things,
hopes all things,
endures all things.
Love never ends . . . .

See 1 Corinthians 13:4–8

TOGETHER EACH DAY

JANUARY

January 1

> We all . . . are changed . . . by the Spirit of the Lord.
>
> 2 Corinthians 3:18

Regardless of the state of your marriage, would you like it to change for the better during the next 365 days? Begin by realizing you can't change the one to whom you said, "I do." The Lord never holds us accountable for the kind of person our partner is. It is a big enough job dealing with ourselves.

You cannot fellowship with Jesus Christ through His Word and through prayer for 365 days and be the same. And in changing you, it just may affect the one you married.

—B.B.

Our prayer for today:

We pray, our Father, that our lives will be completely devoted to You. Change what keeps us from loving You—and each other—as we should.

January 2

> Now you can have real love . . . because your souls have been cleansed from selfishness and hatred when you trusted Christ. . . .
>
> 1 Peter 1:22 LB

For we see marriage as the most exciting and fulfilling of all human relationships. It is the most practical arena of self-discovery, the most basic building block of any society. It is more than a loving, supportive relationship. Marriage brings together two human beings with everything that is theirs. It invites them to contribute whatever they are— and *all* that they are—to a new style of life. Marriage enables a man and a woman to give each other the gift of themselves in a lifelong commitment. It is the place of intimate discovery and sharing in which two people can say, "My lover—my friend."

COLLEEN and LOUIS EVANS, JR.

Our prayer for today:

Our Father, as we give ourselves each day to the other may our relationship become more loving, more understanding.

January 3

Beloved,
let us love one another,
because love takes its origin in God,
and everyone that loves
is a child of God
and knows God.
He who has no love
does not know God,
because God is love.
God's love
was made manifest
among us
by the fact that God
sent his only-begotten Son
into the world
that we might have life
through him.
This loves consists
not in our having loved God

but in his having loved us
and his having sent his Son
as a propitiation
for our sins.
Beloved,
if God so loved us,
we in turn
ought to love one another.

See 1 John 4:7–11

Our prayer for today:

Almighty God, teach us to love You, our Heavenly Father, and each other. Our love is so shallow—so fragile—compared to the deep, everlasting love You have for us. We praise and thank You, Lord.

January 4

Even as the Son of man came not to be ministered unto, but to minister, and to give his life a ransom for many.

Matthew 20:28

"Husbands, love your wives, as Christ loved the church and gave himself up for her."

That is a tremendous sentence. A whole lifetime is not enough to understand the depth of its meaning.

How did Christ love His Church? He served her. He worked for her and helped her. He healed her, comforted her and cleansed her, even washing her feet—and that was the duty of slaves in Jesus' time. The Church was everything to Christ, and He gave her everything, including His life.

Don't you see how God's word becomes a chisel that cuts and hurts us? It cuts more keenly than any two-edged sword. Christ was not what we men like to be—a big chief or a sheik who wants to be served. He was the slave of His Church.

WALTER TROBISCH

Our prayer for today:

In a world, Lord, where the "macho" image so often belies the criteria of real love, help us to look to Jesus Christ for our example.

January 5

Live happily with the woman you love through the fleeting days of life, for the wife God gives you is your best reward down here for all your earthly toil.

Ecclesiastes 9:9 LB

. . . nothing is so important as the "now." *Now* is all we really have —not yesterday, nor tomorrow, but now. ". . . now is the accepted time . . . now is the day of salvation" (2 Corinthians 6:2). It is never too late to make a marriage work, to turn to Christ to be forgiven and strengthened, and to start again.

I know whereof I speak, for I have been through it—through hasty, ill-considered, un-Christian marriage, disillusionment, separation, divorce—but thanks be to God, He finally got through to me, and my heart had its hardness taken away, and my life transformed, and I have known the joy of a *real* marriage. I know now that divorce settles nothing, but that God binding the hearts of man and wife together can settle *anything.*

DALE EVANS ROGERS

Our prayer for today:

Our Lord, take any hardness from our hearts, so that we may know the real joy You intend in our marriage.

January 6

The Lord watches over all the plans and paths of godly men. . . .

Psalms 1:6 LB

I looked into your face and knew
that you were true;
those clear, deep eyes awoke in me
a trust in you.

I'd dreamt of shoulders broad and straight,
one built to lead;
I met you once and knew that you
were all I need.

You did not have to say a word
to make me feel
that will, completely in control,
was made of steel.

I'd dreamt of dashing love and bold,
life wild with zest;
but when with you my heart was stilled
to perfect rest.

And how? I could not understand,
it seemed so odd:
till on my heart it quietly dawned
—love is of God!

RUTH BELL GRAHAM

Our prayer for today:

Dear Father, thank You for this love we have for each other, which comes from You. Together we experience that quiet, joyful assurance that comes from being loved.

January 7

All who listen to my instructions and follow them are wise, like a man who builds his house on solid rock. . . .

Matthew 7:24 LB

The family begins when a man and woman join their lives together in marriage. Everything is at stake in the relationship of that basic pair. If it is a good relationship then that marriage is like a house "built upon a rock" and all the winds and rains of life can beat upon it and it will stand and function and meet the needs of those in it.

There is no way to build a happy, effective family on an inadequate relationship between a husband and wife. It is like building a house "upon the sand" and the pressures and problems which would be handled easily by other families will cause this one to shake and possibly even crumble.

KENNETH CHAFIN

Our prayer for today:

Our Savior, let our relationship always be built on the solid assurance of Your love. When times of difficulty come, all needs will be met in the power of Your strength, Lord Jesus.

January 8

> . . . though your sins be as scarlet, they shall be white as snow. . . .

Isaiah 1:18

There is a story of a physician whose books were examined after he died. It was discovered that a number of the accounts were crossed out and the doctor had written across the page: FORGIVEN—TOO POOR TO PAY. The physician's wife decided that many of these people *could* pay, and so she took some of these accounts to court. The judge asked one question: "Is this your husband's handwriting?" When she replied that it was, he said: "Then there is no tribunal in the land that can obtain this money, when he has written the word *forgiven.*" . . . that story comes from the heart of God. When God says it is forgiven, then it *is* forgiven, and there is no guilt and no liability any longer.

CHARLES L. ALLEN

Our prayer for today:

Thank You, Father, for the love that sent Jesus to die for our sins. May this love check our hearts today, so that we will not sin against You.

January 9

> And thine ears shall hear a word behind thee, saying, This is the
> way, walk ye in it, when ye turn to the right hand, and when ye
> turn to the left.

Isaiah 30:21

It generally comes through your own conscience—a sort of growing
conviction that such and such a course of action is the one He wants
you to take. Or it may be given you in the advice of friends of sound
judgment—those who love you most.

God speaks sometimes through our circumstances and guides us,
closing doors as well as opening them.

He will let you know what you must do, and what you must be. He
is waiting for you to touch Him. The hand of faith is enough. Your
trembling fingers can reach Him as He passes.

> Reach out your faith—touch Him.
> He will not ask, "who touched me?"
> He will know.

PETER MARSHALL

Our prayer for today:

In faith we reach out to You, our Savior, who has touched our lives
with Your love and forgiveness. Keep us open to Your voice, so that
we will be aware of Your guidance, Lord Jesus.

January 10

> And to know the love of Christ, which passeth knowledge, that ye
> might be filled with all the fulness of God.

Ephesians 3:19

In one of William Shakespeare's sonnets, he states: "Love is not love
which alters when it alteration finds." Often, when the one we love
disappoints us or fails to be what we dreamed he or she would be, our

feelings change. The love that was so strong falters, and we look at the other with a critical eye.

During the wedding ceremony of Queen Elizabeth and Prince Philip, the Archbishop of Canterbury said to them, "The ever-living Christ is here to bless you. The nearer you keep to Him, the nearer you will be to each other."

I have found this to be true in my own marriage. It is easier to overlook faults, to forgive, and to love as I should, if my daily walk with Jesus Christ is a close one. As I see how I fail to live up to His yardstick of perfection, my whole attitude changes, and I no longer expect the impossible from my husband. The unchanging love of Jesus Christ for us—even though so many times we fail Him—puts into true perspective the depth of our own love for each other.

—J. W. B.

Our prayer for today:

Lord Jesus, Your example of unselfish, unchanging love makes our love for each other seem so paltry. May we live so close to You, our loving Savior, that our love for each other will deepen each day.

January 11

But remember that in God's plan men and women need each other.

1 Corinthians 11:11 LB

Sex is not the most important thing that makes a marriage work. But it is important. It has no authority of its own. It cannot finally fulfill. In love's highest ecstasies the lover knows that this is not all there is. The closest closeness is not close enough. The "I-thou" that we thought was ultimate brings us ultimately to that other Thou. It is the will of God that leads to freedom. It is the will of God that finally fulfills. "The world and all its passionate desires will one day disappear, but the man who is following God's will is part of the permanent and cannot die."

ELISABETH ELLIOT

Our prayer for today:

Father, our needs are met in You and in each other. Help us to keep all the aspects of our marriage in the right perspective. Thank You for our love, Lord.

January 12

> Seek ye first the kingdom of God, and his righteousness; and all these things shall be added unto you.
>
> Matthew 6:33

Mary Jane and I are growing in the realization that we are fellow adventurers in Christ. Increasingly, he is the center of the relationship. The more we love him more than we love each other, the more we can love and enjoy each other. Our marriage began, really, when we shifted our ultimate loyalty, security, and need to him. Then we could begin to be to each other what he increasingly becomes to us. Neither one of us can love each other as much as we need to be loved. Only Christ can do that! When we allow him to love us, we can free each other to be Christ's persons. Then we have limitless resources of love in him for each other.

LLOYD JOHN OGILVIE

Our prayer for today:

We know, Lord Jesus, we cannot love each other as we should, because we are very human. As we love You and put You first in our lives, we find a liberating love entering our beings. Thank You, that we find it easier to love each other!

January 13

> And all things, whatsoever ye shall ask in prayer, believing, ye shall receive.
>
> Matthew 21:22

How Jesus loved to pray in secret Himself! He had a habit of "rising up a great while before day" and going outdoors—to a mountainside or some other deserted place—to pray. Perhaps because of the small, crowded Palestinian houses, that was the only way He could find privacy and solitude.

Before major decisions—such as His choosing of the twelve apostles—He would pray alone an entire night. And going back to the beginning of His public ministry, we find Jesus going off into the desert for forty days and forty nights of seclusion and concentrated prayer. He knew that power was needed; in secret He would find it.

CATHERINE MARSHALL

Our prayer for today:

Our Lord, in our prayer life we would seek time alone with You. We sense the need to go to a quiet place, so that You are preeminent in our thoughts. Thank You for these times that make the hours together more glorious!

January 14

For thy Maker is thine husband; the Lord of hosts is his name. . . .

Isaiah 54:5

Paul has compared the union between Christ and the church to the marriage relationship. Quoting the words of Jesus, ". . . 'a man shall leave his father and mother and shall be joined to his wife, and the two shall become one flesh,'" Paul says, "It is a great truth that is hidden here. I for my part refer it to Christ and to the church" (Ephesians 5:31, 32 NEB). In the same chapter, Paul tells us that Christ "provides and cares for" the church, "because it is his body, of which we are living parts" (*see* Ephesians 5:29, 30 NEB).

What is your response to all this? What can you do but receive it fully, with all its tremendous possibilities for love and union between you and Jesus? Receive Him as your bridegroom, and seek all the manifestations of His love.

HANNAH WHITALL SMITH
Paraphrased by
CATHERINE JACKSON

Our prayer for today:

Lord Jesus, our union grows more wonderful because You, the Bridegroom of Your church, love us. Your care and provision are more than we deserve, our Lord and our God.

January 15

I was hungry, [and] you gave me food. . . .

Matthew 25:35 NEB

It is the good person, the gracious soul, the generous heart who helps the downtrodden. It is they who go out into a weary old world to bind up broken hearts, set the prisoners free, tend the sin-sick strangers, lift up the fallen, bring the oil of joy to those who mourn, spread light and cheer where darkness descends, feed the hungry, and share the good news of God's gracious love to the lost. . . .

The man or woman who expresses the genuine goodness of a gracious God has nothing to fear, nothing to hide, nothing to protect. There is no need to apologize for his or her performance. It comes flowering like a fresh fruit blossom out of the divine life within, finding its final perfection in rich and ripe maturity of character like Christ's.

W. PHILLIP KELLER

Our prayer for today:

Make us aware, Lord, of the people hurting around us. Let our concern not be perfunctory or self-glorifying. May it be completely guided by Your grace and love.

January 16

> When he, the Spirit of truth, is come, he will guide you into all
> truth. . . .
>
> John 16:13

We can't possibly outgive God. As we make ourselves available to
Him, He allows us to be far more fulfilled and to see greater results than
we possibly could outside His will. God owes no man anything, yet His
rewards are far more fulfilling and satisfying than any we could possibly
imagine. To be available is not always easy, but there is no other way
to achieve a more satisfying and victorious life.

God's plan leaves no room for freak accidents. He has created us as
we are, with a free will to choose, a mind to create, and time to
determine how we will invest our lives even in such a time as this.

VONETTE Z. BRIGHT

Our prayer for today:

Our Lord, may our lives always be available to You. So often we fill
our days with meaningless activities, when we should be serving You.
Forgive our selfishness, Lord.

January 17

> I will give you new and right desires . . . and give you new hearts
> of love. . . .
>
> Ezekiel 36:26 LB

In my work as a marriage counselor, I am frequently surprised at the
naiveté of couples who become disillusioned when the first blush of
romantic emotion has faded. With terrible guilt a woman will say,
"Doctor, I'm afraid I don't love my husband anymore. What's wrong
with me?" Nothing is wrong with her, of course, except that she is
probably spending too much time analyzing her feelings.

The experts at love realize that emotions ebb and flow, and they look
for gestures of love even when their emotions are on the wane. What's

more, they are never content with telling the beloved they care—they show it in small expressions of affection.

ALAN LOY MCGINNIS

Our prayer for today:

Our Father, quite frankly, there are times we do not feel a deep, overwhelming love for each other. Give to our hearts Your tenderness, so that by small gestures of affection we can touch each other with Your love . . . and ours.

January 18

> If we are faithless, He remains faithful; for He cannot deny Himself.
>
> 2 Timothy 2:13 NAS

Because of our relationship with God in Christ, we have confidence in Him and we can trust Him. That is the basis for our future hope. We can be sure that He will not let us down. His promises are trustworthy. And surprisingly, the reverse is true also. God continues to open up and trust *in us,* even when we are unfaithful and we let Him down. As you and I become more and more like the person of Jesus Christ, we become more trustworthy individuals. In other words, people can trust us more, they can have more faith in us.

H. NORMAN WRIGHT
and
REX JOHNSON

Our prayer for today:

Thank You for trusting us, Father. How often we let You down; yet You are always faithful. As we read and meditate upon Your Son, Jesus Christ, we ask that our lives will become more worthy of Your love.

January 19

> Stay always within the boundaries where God's love can reach and
> bless you. . . .

Jude 21 LB

We must never forget that a Christian home is a strategic point for
the enemy. He will do his utmost to attack it, looking for its weak spots
and using them to his advantage. We know how weak we are against
this enemy, but more important, we know that with Jesus we will be
victorious. Jude 21 (LB) tells us always to remain within the boundaries
where God's love can reach and bless us.

CORRIE TEN BOOM

Our prayer for today:

In our homes, Jesus, we find how weak we really are. We pray in
Your name for strength to resist the enemy and keep within Your
sheltering love.

January 20

> . . . he sent away the people. And when he had sent them away,
> he departed into a mountain to pray.

Mark 6:45, 46

Have you considered the cost of praying? Are you aware that meaningful prayer means paying a price? Or, in your prayer life, are you as
casual and hasty as the tourist on a rush tour of Europe who screeched
to a stop in front of Chartres Cathedral, jumped out, and called to his
wife, "You take the inside, I'll do the outside. Meet you here in five
minutes." You will never understand or appreciate praying without a
disciplined and careful effort. After all, you are meant to be embarking
on a relationship, and relationships—especially genuine ones which are
fragile and growing—demand commitment.

WILLIAM P. BARKER

Our prayer for today:

Jesus, we think of the time You spent in prayer. We ask forgiveness for the times we rush through ours. May we set aside the complexities of life and commune with You. Help us to find those moments, Lord.

January 21

Those who still reject me are like the restless sea. . . . There is no peace, says my God, for them!

Isaiah 57:20, 21 LB

We know that we were created with freedom of choice and are responsible for our choices; however, God knows what our choices will be. He doesn't force us, for then there would be no freedom, but it is His will that we accept Him and love Him, because He first loved us.

I believe that God places a man and a woman together, even before they know Him personally, and then will guide their lives if they respond and accept guidance. I think marriages are made in heaven, but can be lived in hell when a man or woman wants to go his or her own way.

CAROLE C. CARLSON

Our prayer for today:

Our Father, we think of the way that, in Your divine wisdom, we were brought together! As we grew up, You were preparing each of our hearts so that one day we would become one. Help us to look to You for guidance, not wanting our separate desires to be granted, but Yours.

January 22

Be careful that none of you fails to respond to the grace of God for if he does there can spring up in him a bitter spirit which can poison the lives of many others.

Hebrews 12:15 PHILLIPS

Christ taught his disciples to deal with their enemies in love. Most of our conflicts are with people much closer to us than enemies. How much more should the difficulties in these relationships be handled in love?

Christ's purpose in his instruction is two-fold. It is his nature to love and he wants his disciples to participate in his nature. Furthermore, learning to act in love rather than reacting in hatred has self-protective qualities.

The poisonous effects of hatred and bitterness have long been recognized. It remains for each one of us to realize that hatred's real victim is the one who is possessed by it. Hatred is a strange poison. It destroys the vessel in which it is stored.

DOUGLAS ROBERTS

Our prayer for today:

Cleanse our hearts from all bitterness and fill them with Your forgiving love, Lord Jesus.

January 23

Behold, I am with thee, and will keep thee in all places whither thou goest. . . .

Genesis 28:15

Even anticipating change is scary. For instance, a woman fears having to move her household again. A man is apprehensive about losing his job. Couples who have never prepared financially for their later years fear the changes they may experience when retirement comes. All of us fear the unknown, but one of the biggest threats to our security is the possibility of things changing. Our stomach knots up within us —as if we were about to come down an uncharted river full of rushing rapids, swirling waters, and unexpected rocks—whenever we anticipate change. Yet being unwilling to change may, in the end, destroy you, taking with it all you really love.

JOYCE LANDORF

Our prayer for today:

Lord, so often there are fears of change, of the unknown. We want to hang on to all that is familiar and dear. Knowing You are with us, wherever we are, in whatever circumstances we find ourselves, gives us courage and strength.

January 24

> And let us not be weary in well doing: for in due season we shall reap, if we faint not.
>
> Galatians 6:9

. . . the tragedy in Christian marriage, as in the Christian life in general, is not that we try and fail or only partially succeed. God is not shocked when we stumble and fall. He knows how weak we are. What breaks His heart is our refusal to get up and keep pressing on toward the mark, our settling for a brown bag lunch when He has filet mignon for us. So don't " . . . be weary in well doing : for in due season we shall reap, if we faint not" (Galatians 6:9).

As His child, put your hand in the hand of God and allow Him to guide you in the art of loving. Even if your marriage isn't a masterpiece, He'll make you a thing of beauty.

PAMELA HEIM

Our prayer for today:

We ask the impossible, Lord: perfection in each other. Help us to examine our own lives and see the imperfections there. Thank You for loving us. May we learn from You to *really* love each other.

January 25

> If any man serve me, let him follow me. . . .
>
> John 12:26

Matthew continued to sit at the receipt of custom until one day the Lord Jesus passed by. He always passes by when there is a hungry soul in need. And what happened? Christ spoke first. If any of us are to come into blessing it must be because the Lord Jesus speaks to us. A mere human voice is of no avail. If we are to enter into a life that is really going to mean victory and power and liberty, it will be because the Lord Jesus speaks to us.

Christ said a very simple word to this man. There was no arguing, there was no reasoning. The Lord Jesus looked at Matthew, and said, "Follow me!" and Matthew, we are told, "left all, rose up and followed Him."

A. LINDSAY GLEGG

Our prayer for today:

May we completely surrender every compartment of our lives to You, Lord Jesus. Each day, let us be aware of Your leading.

January 26

> . . . [love] envieth not; [love] vaunteth not itself, is not puffed up, Doth not behave itself unseemly, seeketh not her own, is not easily provoked, thinketh no evil; Rejoiceth not in iniquity, but rejoiceth in the truth.

1 Corinthians 13:4–6

Love isn't just a kind of soft feeling, a thrill of honeysuckle fragrance while being kissed on a June night. Love isn't just happiness in ideal situations with everything going according to daydreams of family life or married life or parent-child closeness and confidences. Love has *work* to do!

EDITH SCHAEFFER

Our prayer for today:

Dear Father, teach us that it is in the everyday work of living unselfishly that we find our expression of real love.

January 27

> Finally, be ye all of one mind, having compassion one of another, love as brethren, be pitiful, be courteous.

1 Peter 3:8

Marriage is founded on mutual esteem. Courtesy is a support for this esteem. Of course this must spring from a deep inward source. It must not be a hollow ceremony. And yet the outward forms are helpful, and no one should despise good manners in the daily life of married people. They are not a matter of indifference, burdensome, or ridiculous. Carelessness in our dress and speech at home borders upon disrespect. We know that there is a connection between cleanliness of body and purity of soul. Likewise, a disregard of the outward forms of respect easily brings with it a contempt for personal dignity in oneself, and in others.

LARRY CHRISTENSON

Our prayer for today:

Lord, each day help us to show more respect and courtesy to each other. It is so easy to become indifferent to the little things that annoy or hurt.

January 28

> Keep yourselves in the love of God. . . .

Jude 21

Because marriage is such an intimate relationship and our emotions are so deeply involved, we sometimes tend to think that whenever we have a problem, ours is a unique situation. As we read literature from out of the past, we find this sort of thing has been going on for years!

A Quaker gentleman, while on a business trip in the mid-1800s, wrote a long letter to his wife. In it he said:

"Thee knows, though I am cross sometimes, I love thee very much. Now I want to love thee through coming years more if possible than I ever have done, and avoid all cross words and feelings. I think with thy assistance I can improve, and perhaps, My Darling, with our Heavenly Father's help we may do more than we think possible now."

He was right! With our Lord's help, our marriage *can* improve. We just have to be willing to let Him help.

J.W.B

Our prayer for today:

Father, our problems are not unique. There is nothing Your divine help cannot solve. Thank You, Lord, for this assurance.

January 29

Accept life with humility and patience, generously making allowances for each other because you love each other.

Ephesians 4:2 PHILLIPS

Too often marital conflict can be summed up in this: Self is on the throne. But when Jesus reigns in two hearts, conflicts can be resolved under His direction and by means of His power. How much conflict we might eliminate from our marriages if we acted upon the truth that our old self-nature was nailed to Jesus' cross! We need vigilance to observe the ways in which this old self-life of sin and pride seeks to live on in us. By faith we must daily assign that self-life to the grave, and open ourselves to His life of victory.

DWIGHT HERVEY SMALL

Our prayer for today:

Our Father, take away the self in our lives, which so often causes disagreements. Through Your Holy Spirit, we ask You to show us the times when our pride comes between us and You, Lord.

January 30

> . . . he hath sent me to bind up the brokenhearted, to proclaim liberty to the captives, and the opening of the prison to them that are bound.
>
> Isaiah 61:1

A sign on a church bulletin board read, "God can mend a broken heart, if you will give Him all the pieces." God can also mend a broken marriage . . . if you will give Him all the pieces. He can take a shattered marriage and glue it together so perfectly that it will not even show the cracks. He will make it stronger than it was before it shattered. Or He can take a good marriage and make it more beautiful every day.

The secret lies in giving it *all* to Him. And before that can be done with a marriage, it has to be done by the individuals that form the marriage. Perhaps the greatest prayer a wife or husband can pray is, "Lord, save this marriage, *beginning with me!*" Or, "Change this marriage, *beginning with me!*"

JACK and CAROLE MAYHALL

Our prayer for today:

Lord, make our marriage more beautiful—completely void of self-interest. Thank You, Lord, that You can restore marriages—if only everyone would give You all the brokenness! We pray for all those who need the restoration of Your love.

January 31

> That I may know him, and the power of his resurrection. . . .
>
> Philippians 3:10

How many pages of your Bible are unpossessed, unexplored territory? How many of them have never been marked or underlined to show what God means to you? We go over the same portions again and again; we live in simple ABC truths; in John 3 and other such chapters, great and wonderful, indeed, as they are. But whole continents of God's redemptive purpose, revealed for the enlightened mind to discover, to feed upon, and to rejoice in, are left unpossessed. You cannot know Jesus our Lord unless you know Him in His Word. Fellow Christians, venture into some unexplored field in the Word of God, and find what blessing there will be to follow.

ALAN REDPATH

Our prayer for today:

Lord God, we sometimes explore Your Word as if it were a minefield. We are afraid to explore any new territory. Be our Guide, Lord, as we expand our knowledge of the Bible.

FEBRUARY

February 1

> . . . tribulation worketh patience; And patience, experience; and experience, hope.

Romans 5:3, 4

It is good to have a healthy honesty on the part of those married longer years, as they relate that awful moment of anger when the wedding ring was thrown on the floor and rolled into a crack and took two hours to find and put back on. It is good for the ones married just a short time to know that a marriage can weather "down" moments and rough places, as well as coming to know that it is important to *work* at relationships with some measure of unselfishness and understanding because the end product is worth it!

EDITH SCHAEFFER

Our prayer for today:

Our Lord, use the moments of anger and hurt constructively in our lives. If someone else's marriage can be helped by our being honest about ours, we thank You for all the rough times we have known!

February 2

> . . . there is sin in their homes, and they are polluted to the depths of their souls. But I will call upon the Lord to save me—and he will.

Psalms 55:15, 16 LB

The broken home has become the number one social problem of America, and could ultimately lead to the destruction of our civilization. Since the basic unity of any society is the home, when the home begins to break, the society is on the way to disintegration. Just as Communism, it is a threat to the American way of life. It does not make screaming headlines; but, like termites, it is eating away at the heart and core of the American structure. It is high time that our so-called experts on marriage, the family, and the home, turn to the Bible. We have read newspaper columns and listened to counselors on the radio; psychiatrists have had a land-office business. In it all, the One who performed the first marriage in the Garden of Eden and instituted the union between man and wife has been left out.

BILLY GRAHAM

Our prayer for today:

Let us not leave You out of our home, Lord Jesus. May we always be conscious of Your love and leading. Forgive us for the times we have forgotten.

February 3

> . . . to give unto them beauty for ashes, the oil of joy for mourning,
> the garment of praise for the spirit of heaviness. . . .

Isaiah 61:3

Know this! Christ never takes our joy away. He gives joy! He says that He came not only to give us life, but give it to us more abundantly! God tells us that the way of the transgressor is hard, but His ways are ways of pleasantness and all His paths are peace.

The joy that the Lord gives is marvelous. It springs up in sorrow and in trouble like a palm tree springing up in a desert.

HENRIETTA MEARS

Our prayer for today:

Your joy is deep within us, Lord Jesus. When the world is dark and there is seemingly no answer to problems, we will remember Your joy is always with us, to comfort and to strengthen.

February 4

> Let us love one another: for love is of God. . . .
>
> 1 John 4:7

I love you, not only for what you are, but for what I am when I am with you. I love you, not only for what you made of yourself, but for what you are making of me.

I love you for the part of me that you bring out.

I love you for putting your hand into my heaped-up heart, and passing over all the foolish, weak things that you can't help dimly seeing there, and for drawing out into the light all the beautiful belongings that no one else had looked quite far enough to find.

I love you because you are helping me to make of the lumber of my life not a tavern, but a temple; out of the works of my every day not a reproach, but a song. . . .

You have done it without a touch, without a word, without a sign. You have done it by being yourself.

ROY CROFT

Our prayer for today:

Thank You, Lord, for the love we two share. May it deepen as the years continue to go by, strengthened and cherished by the enormity of Your abiding love.

February 5

> Keep yourselves in the love of God. . . .
>
> Jude 21

Some people seem to think of God's love as being totally different from human love—somehow less personal and less real. But if ever human love was tender, self-sacrificing, and devoted, divine love is infinitely more so, and infinitely more forgiving, more willing to suffer for its loved ones, and more eager to lavish the best gifts and blessings upon them. Put together all the tenderest love you know of—the deepest you have ever felt and the greatest that has ever been given you; heap upon it all the love of all the loving human hearts in the world; multiply it by infinity. Only then will you *begin* to have some faint idea of the love of God in Christ Jesus.

HANNAH WHITALL SMITH
Paraphrased by
CATHERINE JACKSON

Our prayer for today:

Our Heavenly Father, because of the deep love we have for each other, we comprehend a fraction of the magnitude of Your love, which surrounds us each day. Because of this incredible knowledge, our hearts rejoice, and we praise You!

February 6

I advise you to obey only the Holy Spirit's instructions. He will tell you where to go and what to do, and then you won't always be doing the wrong things your evil nature wants you to.

Galatians 5:16 LB

You and I are living in rough times. We must make our way through minefields of evil, booby traps of deception, brush fires of sickness and disease, wastelands of economic disaster, burning deserts of disappointment. "I won't take you out of this world," Jesus told us, "But don't be afraid, because I've overcome that world of dangers. All power is Mine. I promise to be with you always."

"How, Lord? How are You with us?"

"Through the Helper."

It is true. He is here. We who in moments of desperation have asked, "What can I do? What is there left?" have felt His answering presence and experienced His help . . . We know now . . . always He holds out to us the exciting promise of something more.

CATHERINE MARSHALL

Our prayer for today:

Thank You, Lord Jesus, for the knowledge that whatever we have to face, we are not alone. Your Holy Spirit is guiding us, giving us wisdom and courage to combat the problems of this life.

February 7

For we know in part. . . .

1 Corinthians 13:9

1 Corinthians 13 has been called the most beautiful combination of words ever written on love. You will note that the only phrase repeated in that chapter is "We know in part."

That is a wonderful fact for which we can thank our Creator. He made us this way. So there are vast ranges of undiscovered terrain waiting for those who begin this trip together. No couple, going at it right, could ever possibly exhaust the faraway places. This is like climbing mountains. You make it to the top of one, and you see more to be explored in the distance.

We can tell you this goes on at least thirty-five years. And we fully expect that it goes on forever and forever. That is some kind of exciting, isn't it?

To do it the way we do it calls for a definite time commitment. We have agreed to spend fifteen minutes a day at this. Fifteen minutes to talk about what's going on inside Charlie and Martha. Sometimes it's mostly monologue, depending on who's hurting. Then again it could be a rapid exchange or slow dredging up of some ancient fear. Often we go beyond the prescribed time. Many of our happiest memories have come from these moments.

CHARLIE W. SHEDD

Our prayer for today:

Father, help us to know each other's needs. May we be people who really *listen* and care.

February 8

> . . . your Father knoweth that ye have need of these things.

> Luke 12:30

Many of us have experienced that again and again God has controlled us through money matters. When we have been in the center of
his will, supplies have been sure; but as soon as we have been out of
vital touch with him, they have become uncertain.

In his own work God must have the sole direction. At times we have
fancied God would have us do a certain thing, but he has showed us
it was not his will by withholding the financial means to do it. So we
have been held under the constant direction of the Lord, and such
direction is most precious.

WATCHMAN NEE

Our prayer for today:

Thank You, Father, for all that You provide for us. We are completely dependent on You for all our needs. May we never forget this,
as we keep our eyes on You.

February 9

> So ought men to love their wives as their own bodies. He that
> loveth his wife loveth himself.

> Ephesians 5:28

St. Paul talks of married people loving each other as they love their
own bodies. This means that, in relation to each other, they have put
away shame and false modesty about bodily functions or bodily
blemishes. They have accepted each other as they have had to accept
themselves—as they are. They have identified themselves with one
another, so that each partner naturally strives to ease pain and discom-
fort in the other as if it were a personal experience. As Edward Carpen-

ter put it, a husband or wife should be a person "whose body is as dear to one, in every part, as one's own."

DAVID R. MACE

Our prayer for today:

When either of us hurts, or is sick, or needs comfort, we pray for Your compassion and love in our hearts, Lord Jesus.

February 10

Use hospitality one to another. . . .

1 Peter 4:9

"Hospitality with a purpose" is a form of Christian service that has its origin in the church, is based on the home, and is pointed toward reaching people. Christians often think their home is not good enough to entertain in, but other people aren't primarily interested in your furnishings or in the refreshments you serve. They will love you for including them as your guests. That's why this kind of ministry can be so effective—because of the need for love and acceptance. More people are won to Christ through love than through logic.

TIM and BEV LAHAYE

Our prayer for today:

Father, let us not make excuses for our home or forget to entertain those You would have for our guests. Your love envelops us, Lord. May we always be ready to share Your love with others in our home.

February 11

And the apostles said unto the Lord, Increase our faith.

Luke 17:5

Faith is a gift of God. It is not, never was, and never will be a product of man's best efforts. It is a gift.

Scripture taught me that Jesus Christ is the author and finisher of our faith—faith comes by hearing; by hearing the Word of God. God healed me by His Word and in His Word I learned why something really wonderful had happened when I turned my life over to Jesus Christ.

In contemplating the imperfection of God's heroic saints, one principle undergirds each study: We may hope to run with feet of clay because Jesus Christ is who He is, has done what He has done, is doing what He is doing, and will do what He will do.

Every assurance the Christian holds is securely rooted in the character of God. That's the reason the comfort of God is based on His faithfulness and not ours.

JEANNETTE CLIFT

Our prayer for today:

Thank You, Lord, that we do not have to rely on our imperfect lives, but on *Your* perfect one! May our faith in You increase each day, as we read Your Word.

February 12

. . . The effectual fervent prayer of a righteous man availeth much.

James 5:16

Prayer constantly enlarges our horizon and our person. It draws us out of the narrow limits within which our habits, our past and our whole personage confine us. Sometimes we receive a clear command, whose implications we do not usually at first understand. It is only afterwards, as we look back over the road we have travelled, that we see that God had a purpose for us, and that he has compelled us to follow it in spite of ourselves.

PAUL TOURNIER

Our prayer for today:

As we pray, Lord, thank You for broadening our vision, so that we may minister in Your name.

February 13

> Be full of love for others, following the example of Christ. . . .

> Ephesians 5:2 LB

The spectrum of love has nine ingredients:
Patience . . . Love suffereth long.
Kindness . . . And is kind.
Generosity . . . Love envieth not.
Humility . . . Love vaunteth not itself, is not puffed up.
Courtesy . . . Doth not behave itself unseemly.
Unselfishness . . . Seeketh not its own.
Good temper . . . Is not provoked.
Guilelessness . . . Taketh not account of evil.
Sincerity . . . Rejoiceth not in unrighteousness, but rejoiceth with the
    truth.
Patience, kindness, generosity, humility, courtesy, unselfishness, good temper, guilelessness, sincerity—these make up the supreme gift, the stature of the perfect man.

HENRY DRUMMOND

Our prayer for today:

Dear Father, may these attributes of love be so imprinted on our hearts and minds that each day we will live closer to You and to each other.

February 14

> . . . for love is strong as death. . . .

> Song of Solomon 8:6

How do I love thee? Let me count the ways.
I love thee to the depth and breadth and height
My soul can reach, when feeling out of sight
For the ends of Being and ideal Grace.
I love thee to the level of everyday's

Most quiet need, by sun and candle-light.
I love thee freely, as men strive for Right;
I love thee purely, as they turn from Praise.
I love thee with the passion put to use
In my old griefs, and with my childhood's faith.
I love thee with a love I seemed to lose
With my lost saints,—I love thee with the
    breath,
Smiles, tears, of all my life!—and, if God choose,
I shall but love thee better after death.

                    ELIZABETH BARRETT BROWNING

Our prayer for today:

Today, let our love shine more brightly, Lord, when we think of all we mean to each other because of You. Our days are numbered by Your loving will, so let us not be afraid to tell each other of our love.

February 15

But God showed his great love for us by sending Christ to die for us while we were still sinners.

                                    Romans 5:8 LB

We manifest a patient love when we, like Jesus Christ, accept our spouses as they are and give them space and time to overcome their areas of imperfection. Or when we find inner peace to express love even if the weaknesses persist through a lifetime. Gibson Winter said: "Acceptance in marriage is the power to love someone and receive him in the very moment that we realize how far he (or she) falls short of our hopes. It is love between two people who see clearly that they do not measure up to one another's dreams. Acceptance is loving the real person to whom one is married. Acceptance is giving up dreams for reality."

                                    PAMELA HEIM

Our prayer for today:

Help each of us, Lord, to give the other breathing space, so that we may overcome the many imperfections in our lives. We ask for Your grace to overlook the faults and love each other truly, Lord.

February 16

> . . . Don't let the sun go down with you still angry—get over it quickly.
>
> Ephesians 4:26 LB

"I love him, Lord, but he drives me bananas!" This was a prayer that came from me, quite involuntarily, after Bill had left for work one morning. His ideas had not agreed with mine. It was not the first time in our marriage we had clashed, and I am sure as Bill drove to work on the freeway, the steering wheel was gripped *extremely* tightly as he told the Lord, "That woman is *impossible!*"

When Bill returned home that evening, we laughed about our argument. We could see how ridiculous it was—blown out of all proportion. During our marriage we have always tried to resolve our differences before we go to sleep at night. It has not always been easy! Sometimes we have only reached the point of agreeing to disagree, but we have always been able to say, "I love you" before turning out the light.

As we have prayed together, or separately, the Lord has given us His grace to forgive and be more pliable to each other's wishes.

—J.W.B

Our prayer for today:

Father, thank You for Your grace, which enables us to overcome our differences.

February 17

> If we say that we have not sinned, we make him a liar, and his word is not in us.
>
> 1 John 1:10

Of all the children the devil has in the world, I believe he loves his pharisaical children most. I was walking with one of them some time ago, and was asked where the Pharisees lived, and I told him, "They live everywhere." Some people think they lived only in the times of the apostles, but not so. If you want to know what a Pharisee is, he is a pretender who talks about keeping the law of God, but does not know it spiritually.

GEORGE WHITEFIELD

Our prayer for today:

Lord, often we are so pharisaical. Help us to see ourselves as *You* see us, and forgive our sins, we pray.

February 18

. . . Worthy is the Lamb . . . to receive power, and riches, and wisdom, and strength, and honour, and glory, and blessing.

Revelation 5:12

In the altar area of Our Lady's Church in Copenhagen, Denmark, you may see the famous statue of Christ carved by Bertel Thorwaldsen. To appreciate fully the significance of the magnificent piece of sculpture, however, you must kneel at the feet of the statue and look up into the face. Perhaps Thorwaldsen intended this as a parable. You must kneel and look up before you can adore. To understand God, you must first *stand under* Jesus Christ. This is adoration.

WILLIAM P. BARKER

Our prayer for today:

We kneel at Your feet, Lord Jesus, asking only to love You as we should.

February 19

> . . . Set thine house in order. . . .
>
> 2 Kings 20:1

Recently a judge, when counselling with a young couple who were asking for a divorce, suggested that they "kiss and make up." "Here and now?" the young man asked incredulously. "Yes, here and now," said the judge. "Do you know of a better time or place?" Well, the young man did kiss his wife, and their hard and drawn faces softened once more and their long pent-up love for each other was no longer withheld. Then the judge said something which might not be expected to be heard in judicial chambers: "The trouble with too many young married couples is that they don't express their love often enough."

If there is to be peace among the nations and among the races of men, it will have to come through homes where patterns of harmony have replaced notes of discord.

CHARLES L. ALLEN
and
CHARLES L. WALLIS

Our prayer for today:

Lord Jesus, take away any pride or stubbornness that comes between us. May expressions of love—a hand on our shoulder, a tender kiss, a gentle touch—tell each how much the other cares.

February 20

> For the power of the life-giving Spirit—and this power is mine through Christ Jesus—has freed me from the vicious circle of sin and death.
>
> Romans 8:2 LB

We all love a victory, whether it be the high-school student watching a football game, the housewife whose cake has risen especially high, or the businessman who closes a profitable business transaction.

Yet for too many Christians, *spiritual* victory is of little concern. The above Scripture indicates that nothing short of a steady and lasting victory is God's norm for every Christian. To be defeated is abnormal.

Since Christ lives in each one of us who has accepted Him as Savior, no enemy is too powerful, no temptation need triumph. Daily victory can be ours by renouncing the sin that has caused defeat and by faith letting God's Spirit have control of our lives, working through us.

First Corinthians 15:57 assures us: "But thanks be to God, which giveth us the victory through our Lord Jesus Christ."

—B.B.

Our prayer for today:

Thank You, Father, that victory in our Christian experience is ours as we fully commit our ways to You. Forgive us when we don't depend on You as we should.

February 21

. . . God . . . grant you to be of the same mind with one another. . . .

Romans 15:5 NAS

When we allow our *emotions* to dominate rational thinking, we have become slaves to our feelings, instead of searchers of facts. A marriage is not built upon just feelings; if it were, we would all give up when we didn't feel like being married! Proverbs gives us this principle:

> By wisdom a house is built,
> And by understanding it is established;
> And by knowledge the rooms are filled
> With all precious and pleasant riches.

Proverbs 24:3, 4 NAS

CAROLE C. CARLSON

Our prayer for today:

Dear Lord, there are days when our emotions spill over and words are flung irresponsibly at the one we love in You. Give us Your love and wisdom to go to each other and gently say, "I am sorry." Our marriage means more to us than false pride or retribution.

February 22

> . . . continue to show deep love for each other, for love makes up
> for many of your faults.
>
> 1 Peter 4:8 LB

The forgiving person is sometimes caricatured as weak and spineless, but just the opposite is true. One must be strong to forgive, for forgiveness is a very positive force. It changes both you and your beloved.

The sad thing about hate, on the other hand, is what it can do to the hater. I talked with a young mother who was bristling with bitterness. Her husband's parents had said some unkind things to her, there had been a bad scene, and she said, "I'll never feel the same toward my in-laws again. Oh, they've apologized, but I can't forget what they've said."

I felt sorry for that woman, for she was the one who was suffering most from her hatred, not her in-laws. In fact, the dangerous thing about bitterness, slander, wrath, malice, and the whole cargo which St. Paul urges us to jettison (Ephesians 4:31, 32) is that these attitudes eat away at us like acid. Not only does our bitterness slop out on those around us and corrode our relationships, it also eats away at our own souls.

ALAN LOY MCGINNIS

Our prayer for today:

Dear Lord, there are times when we have been mistreated—misunderstood by someone. Emotions rise up inside us, and we feel as if we'll never love or forgive that person again. Lord Jesus, it is only Your forgiveness in our hearts that will neutralize the acidic, demeaning thoughts we carry within. Cleanse us from all this, we pray.

February 23

And to know the love of Christ, which passeth knowledge, that ye
might be filled with all the fulness of God.

Ephesians 3:19

If somebody asks me, "How does my heart expand to receive more
and more of Jesus?" my answer is this: The capacity to receive the grace
of God and the indwelling of His Holy Spirit is measured by the
character of your obedience and your faith. If you want more of Him,
then cut down the dead wood. Get rid of the thing that robs you of your
victory, and grace will be poured into your life.

For the greater the obedience, the greater the discipline, the greater
the faith, the fuller and more complete the allegiance to our precious
Lord, the more does the heart expand to receive more and more of
Jesus.

ALAN REDPATH

Our prayer for today:

Lord, enlarge our hearts as we empty them of selfish desires. Fill
them with Your Holy Spirit, so that we may obey and serve You, Lord
Jesus.

February 24

Love each other with brotherly affection and take delight in honoring each other.

Romans 12:10 LB

Affection between husband and wife can be a honeymoon or a hell.
The Bible says, "Husbands, love your wives." Affection is a spiritual
and a biological need. The wife is to show her affection by responding
to the God-like love of her husband.

Being in love is not primarily sexual. Sex is a part of love but surely
not the whole of love. The concept you hold of affection, or of being
in love, will have a direct bearing on your success and personal satisfac-

tion. Affection is attractive, but be careful you attract the right person. Of all the emotions in the human body, none seems as right as affection. It can at times feel divine. That's what makes it dangerous.

If the love-desire, the feeling of affection, is allowed to have its way unconditionally, it can become a demon. But set affection in a proper relationship between husband and wife or between friends of mutual respect and interest, and you have found the nearest thing to grace.

DON H. POLSTON

Our prayer for today:

Lord, may our affection for each other be controlled by You. Out of it may we each learn what it is to give lovingly. May our love not consume or be fraught with jealousy. Fill us with a deep respect for each other, Lord Jesus.

February 25

. . . I will never leave thee, nor forsake thee.

Hebrews 13:5

Could it be that God seems distant to you right now? Perhaps He does not seem to be your Guide, your Strength, your Wisdom and your all. . . .

You may feel He is far away but the truth is, He is near . . . more real than the pain you are enduring. He longs to support you in the crucible of crisis. Trust Him today. Like a child, look up into the Father's face. His arms are open, not closed. His Son, Jesus Christ, is ready to enter your life if you will only invite Him to do so. Right now.

He will hear you.

He has a special love . . . for those who hurt.

CHARLES R. SWINDOLL

Our prayer for today:

When we hurt, Lord, we remember You are near. Your presence envelops us, and we know You are watching over us. Our feelings fluctuate, but Your love is steady and constant.

February 26

Jesus wept.

John 11:35

There are few people on the face of the earth who have not suffered heartbreak at one time or another. Some disappointment, some injury, some frustration has left a scar upon their lives that seems ineradicable. Every one carries the memory of some bitter sorrow or of some shattered hope of the past. It may have been assuaged by the passage of time, or it may have left a wound that is irremediable. Whatever the nature of the trouble, Jesus was sent to aid the brokenhearted, and so are his servants. We must walk the road to Galilee with him if we would fulfil our mission.

MERRILL C. TENNEY

Our prayer for today:

Help us to see others through Your eyes, Lord Jesus, so that we, too, may weep with them, having Your compassion in our hearts. May we not judge or preach, but love and help heal the heartaches of our neighbors.

February 27

Now the God of peace. . . . Make you perfect in every good work to do his will. . . .

Hebrews 13:20, 21

Not all of us are called to minister far from home. Around us in our communities are people who need Him. Our compassion, brought about by His Holy Spirit, can reach out to those who have lost hope and who desperately seek an answer to their seemingly unsolvable problems. Ministering through Him we avoid the ego trip that can so easily become our incentive, instead of wanting to glorify Him.

His hand is still reaching out to transform lives. He takes us, even if our faith is as small as "a grain of mustard seed," then helps us grow each day to the full beauty of discipleship.

—J.W.B.

Our prayer for today:

Lord, make us channels of Your compassion. Our faith is small, Lord, and we feel inadequate to cope with the need around us. We look to You as we minister in Your name.

February 28

> And hope maketh not ashamed; because the love of God is shed abroad in our hearts by the Holy Ghost which is given unto us.
>
> Romans 5:5

The relevance of the Gospel to the problem of love has been rooted by many writers. One of the unique features of Christianity is that it makes loving possible in the very face of rejection and persecution. In fact, central to the whole Christian understanding of love is the idea that love is only meaningful in the face of opposition and dislike. Jesus said, "For if ye love them which love you, what thank have ye? for sinners also love those that love them" (Luke 6:32 KJV). The call here is clearly to a much higher form of love, a love that transcends barriers of hate, dislike, fear, and indifference. This is a love that has no desire for personal reward—knowing full well that all the reward that love has to offer is in its giving and not its receiving.

ARCHIBALD D. HART

Our prayer for today:

Our Father, we would love in such an unselfish way that we would not expect to be loved in return. When we are rejected or badly treated, help us to keep Jesus Christ's love in our hearts for those who offend us.

February 29

> . . . behold, now is the accepted time; behold, now is the day of salvation.

> 2 Corinthians 6:2

The thought of living moment by moment is of such central importance. . . . And to all who desire to learn the blessed art of living only a moment at a time, we want to say: The way to learn it is to exercise yourself in living in the present moment. Each time your attention is free to occupy itself with the thought of Jesus—whether it be with time to think and pray, or only for a few passing seconds—let your first thought be to say: Now, at this moment, I do abide in Jesus. Use such time, not in vain regrets that you have not been abiding fully, or still more hurtful fears that you will not be able to abide, but just at once take the position the Father has given you: "I am in Christ; this is the place God has given me. I accept it; here I rest; I do now abide in Jesus." This is the way to learn to abide continually.

ANDREW MURRAY

Our prayer for today:

Living Lord, may we become more and more aware of Your presence, so we will learn to live free of fear of the future.

MARCH

March 1

> You husbands should try to understand the wives you live with. . . .
>
> 1 Peter 3:7 PHILLIPS

Husbands may well ask, "Why does God command me four times to love my wife and only once direct her to love me?" That is a question I have pondered for many years and can offer two possible answers. First, women have a greater need to be loved. As one woman said, "Without love I have no life!" Second, men have a harder time loving. Because of their nature, women possess an enormous capacity for love, whereas men have to cultivate theirs. That is why a man should be very careful about walking in the control of the Spirit. He needs the supernatural love of God to be the lifetime lover God commands him to be, and that his wife naively expected him to be when she agreed to become his wife.

TIM and BEV LAHAYE

Our prayer for today:

You brought us together, Lord, knowing our natures were different. Thank You, that through Your Holy Spirit, we can be satisfied by giving true love to each other.

March 2

. . . whosoever will lose his life for my sake shall find it.

Matthew 16:25

All my life I labored for success, wealth, acceptance and power. The more I obtained, the less I discovered I had. Surrendering everything in absolute brokenness, however, was the beginning of finding the identity and purpose for which I had battled so hard. In giving up my life to Christ I had found it. . . .

"Dying to self," "honest repentance," and "taking up the cross" are phrases that so many new believers find to be incomprehensible or once comprehended, painful and hence forgettable. No one wants to "lose" his life or suffer as Christ did. The verses we Christians choose to remember are the promises of what God will do for us, not the conditions He demands in return.

CHARLES W. COLSON

Our prayer for today:

We cling to our paltry possessions, Lord, not wanting to surrender all we have to You. Forgive us, we pray. Help us, Lord Jesus, to be worthy followers—completely and utterly dead to self.

March 3

The foundation of God standeth sure. . . .

2 Timothy 2:19

Because God chose me to inherit all the riches He has promised His children (Ephesians 1:11) . . .
• *Therefore,* I can claim His wisdom (James 1:5) when my mother-in-law wants to come and live with us for an extended visit.
Because God loved me so much that He gave me a new life and saved me, not "as a result of works, that no one should boast" (Ephesians 2:9), but as a free gift . . .
• *Therefore,* I can love my father-in-law when he questions my judg-

ment in choosing a place to live or accepting a new job.

Because Christ preached peace and gave me open access to speak to the God of this entire universe . . .

• *Therefore,* I can claim that peace when my heart is in turmoil over something thoughtless I have said or done.

Because God forgave me for all my sins, past, present, and future, when Christ bore them on the cross . . .

• *Therefore,* I can walk in love and forgive my in-laws (or any others) when they injure me, either purposely or unjustifiably.

CAROLE C. CARLSON

Our prayer for today:

Our Father, there are times in both our lives when our loved ones say or do something that really annoys or hurts us. Help us to treat them lovingly, putting ourselves in their position. Sometimes it is so hard to do! Thank You for Your grace when we have reacted thoughtlessly.

March 4

. . . Come home with me, and refresh thyself. . . .

1 Kings 13:7

When I first visited the home of Dr. and Mrs. Nelson Bell, the parents of Mrs. Billy Graham, I sensed a warmth—a feeling that love was pre-eminent. As I watched the tender way this couple responded to each other, I saw the reason their home was so welcoming. Through their love for Jesus Christ and each other, the joy of their caring spilled over to everyone who came through their front door. Visitors left encouraged and refreshed, ready to face their own particular problems.

Victor Hugo wrote, in his poem "House and Home":

A house is built of logs and stone,
Of tiles and post and piers;
A home is built of loving deeds
That stand a thousand years.

Both Dr. and Mrs. Bell are now with the Lord, but the memory of their home nestled in the mountains of North Carolina lives on as a reminder of what a house, an apartment, or even a room, can become if the occupants reflect the beauty of Jesus Christ.

—J.W.B.

Our prayer for today:

May people sense who is head of our home, Lord, and knowing, be renewed with Your love.

March 5

> . . . I am come that they might have life, and that they might have it more abundantly.

> John 10:10

Romance is not made of shivers and tingles—in spite of what the movies may tell us! Romance is not even what we do—or don't do. Doing the right things may enhance romance, but basically romance is an attitude. It is a man and woman being alive to one another—not taking one another for granted. It is an atmosphere—a look that speaks more eloquently than words, a squeeze of the hand as you pass each other in a crowded room, a pat on the head or the shoulder for no particular reason. Romance is an element of fascination and delight that culminates in a deep desire to experience all of life with the one we love.

Romance helps make marriage the triumph it can be . . . a triumph that is both a gift from God, and one that "takes *some* doing."

COLLEEN and LOUIS EVANS, JR.

Our prayer for today:

Thank You, God, for the romance in our marriage; for the times we share intimate moments; for the joy of nearness, even when we are apart; for a look that says, "I love you," bringing the warmth of Your love into our lives.

March 6

> For whosoever shall do the will of God, the same is my brother, and my sister, and mother.

> Mark 3:35

God's will for us is not only more loving than a father's; it is more tender than a mother's. It is true that God does oftentimes revolutionize utterly our life plans when we surrender ourselves to His will. It is true that He does sometimes require of us things that to others seem hard. But when the will is once surrendered, the revolutionized life plans become just the plans that are most pleasant, and the things that to others seem hard, are just the things that are easiest and most delightful. Do not let Satan deceive you into being afraid of God's plans for your life.

R. A. TORREY

Our prayer for today:

Lord, *our* wills often get in the way of Your purpose for our lives. Forgive us for settling for so much less than You are desirous of sharing with us.

March 7

> Thy word is a lamp unto my feet, and a light unto my path.

> Psalms 119:105

Many persons make the mistake of thinking they can measure the certainty of their salvation by their feelings. It is the Word of God that is their foundation and therefore it is essential for the new convert in Christ to have a practical knowledge of the Bible. More than anyone else it is the new convert who will come under the fire of the enemy. He needs the knowledge of the Sword of the Spirit. As the Lord Jesus used this Sword to overcome the evil one in His temptation experiences, so we must learn to defend ourselves against every sort of attack.

CORRIE TEN BOOM

Our prayer for today:

Our Father, by Your Holy Spirit, help us to learn more of Your Word. May we be armed against all the battles we will face.

March 8

> . . . he hath sent me to heal the brokenhearted. . . .

>   Luke 4:18

God-love will cause you to forgive all past and present sins committed by your spouse and ask God to enable you to forget. In my own experience, the longer I fret, fume and fuss about a thing, the more firmly it becomes lodged in my mind. On the contrary, it seems the quicker I forgive a real or imagined wrong, the more easily the incident is forgotten. If, however, the memory does remain, I find it amazing that God has healed the hurt caused by the forgiven incident.

PAMELA HEIM

Our prayer for today:

Father, take away the thoughts and differences that would mar our marriage. May we learn to forgive and forget and love as You do, Lord.

March 9

> . . . for God is love.

>   1 John 4:8

The Glory of Life is to love,
Not to be loved,
To give, not to get,

To serve, not to be served,
To be a strong hand in the dark to another in the time of
    need,
To be a cup of strength to any soul in a crisis of
    weakness.
This is to know The Glory of Life.

AUTHOR UNKNOWN

Our prayer for today:

As we contemplate Your love, Father, we realize ours is so fragmentary. Teach us the wholeness of abiding, selfless love: love that reaches out and bears our loved one through all the joys, trials, and heartaches of life.

March 10

. . . when troubles come. . . . sing his praises with much joy.

Psalms 27:5,6 LB

In the case of adversity or difficult circumstances we want "out." Looking for the nearest exit, we duck and dodge to free ourselves from any unpleasant situation. We even pray earnestly to be delivered from every difficult or demanding experience.

All of this is the opposite of love in action. Love means I will push on in spite of obstacles. Love means being willing to suffer and endure the slings and stones of life. And love perseveres against formidable odds, just simply "keeping on."

W. PHILLIP KELLER

Our prayer for today:

Our Heavenly Father, let us, like David, learn to praise You in the midst of heartache. It is not always easy, Lord. We would rather praise You for our joys. In the valleys, we still find Your love, and it is there we know the meaning of *real* joy!

March 11

> Therefore as the church is subject unto Christ, so let the wives be
> to their own husbands in every thing. Husbands, love your wives,
> even as Christ also loved the church, and gave himself for it.
>
> Ephesians 5:24, 25

In every Christian marriage the world should be able to see that
mutual giving and self-giving which characterize the relationship between Christ and the Church.

What opportunities present themselves daily to the man to give—to
express toward his mate the love of One who gave up His very life for
His Bride! What opportunities present themselves daily to the woman
to give—to express the faithfulness of the Church as it is described in
Ephesians 5:24 and 27, ". . . subject in everything to Christ . . . without
spot or wrinkle, holy and without blemish!" This is not merely an ideal,
but is the projected goal of the Holy Spirit with every Christian couple.

LARRY CHRISTENSON

Our prayer for today:

Let others see in our marriage an accord that springs from being
subject to You, Lord Jesus. When we give to each other, we find the
glorious fulfillment of marriage, as You designed it.

March 12

> Say to them that are of a fearful heart, Be strong, fear not. . . .
>
> Isaiah 35:4

The crosses which we make for ourselves by a restless anxiety as to
the future, are not crosses which come from God. We show want of
faith in Him by our false wisdom, wishing to forestall His arrange-
ments, and struggling to supplement His Providence by our own providence. The future is not yet ours; perhaps it never will be. If it comes,
it may come wholly different from what we have foreseen. Let us shut
our eyes, then, to that which God hides from us, and keeps in reserve

in the treasures of His deep counsels. Let us worship without seeing; let us be silent; let us abide in peace.

FRANÇOIS DE FÉNELON

Our prayer for today:

Lord, forgive our anxiety for the future. May we learn to live a day at a time, confident of Your love and concern for every detail of our lives.

March 13

Bread corn is bruised . . . .

Isaiah 28:28

Many of us cannot be used to become food for the world's hunger until we are broken in Christ's hands. "Bread corn is bruised." Christ's blessing ofttimes means sorrow, but even sorrow is not too great a price to pay for the privilege of touching other lives with benediction. The sweetest things in this world today have come to us through tears and pain.

J. R. MILLER

Our prayer for today:

The human in us, Lord, shrinks from being "bruised." We long for an easy life. But, Lord Jesus, if through sorrow we may be able to reach out to others, we thank You for all the tears, all the pain.

March 14

Yet those who wait for the Lord will gain new strength . . . They will walk and not become weary.

Isaiah 40:31 NAS

One night I had a dream—I dreamed I was walking along the beach with the Lord and across the sky flashed scenes from my life. For each scene I noticed two sets of footprints in the sand; one belonged to me and the other to the Lord. When the last scene of my life flashed before us, I looked back at the footprints in the sand. I noticed that many times along the path of my life there was only one set of footprints. I also noticed that it happened at the very lowest and saddest times in my life. This really bothered me, and I questioned the Lord about it.

"Lord, You said that once I decided to follow You, You would walk with me all the way. But I have noticed that during the most troublesome times in my life there is only one set of footprints. I don't understand why in times when I need You most, You should leave me."

The Lord replied, "My precious, precious child, I love you, and I would never, never leave you during your times of trials and suffering. When you see only one set of footprints, it was then I carried you."

AUTHOR UNKNOWN

Our prayer for today:

Thank You, Father, for Your strength so generously supplied in our times of weakness. Your abiding presence is our assurance of Your constant love.

March 15

Ye are the light of the world. A city that is set on an hill cannot be hid.

Matthew 5:14

On Sir Christopher Wren's memorial in St. Paul's Cathedral there are these words: "If you seek a monument, look around you." If you seek a monument to the power of the Gospel, look around you at the changed lives of God's people. That is the outward evidence of the value of the message we preach. The ultimate evidence of the all-sufficiency of Christ is seen in the changed, transformed lives of His people. And that is what the world is waiting to see. I believe there are very many hungry people today, ready for the message of the Gospel if they could only see the power of it in your life and mine.

A. LINDSAY GLEGG

Our prayer for today:

Lord Jesus, fill our hearts with the light of Your Holy Spirit, so that others will see the power and be drawn to You.

March 16

The eyes of the Lord run to and fro throughout the whole earth, to shew himself strong in the behalf of them whose heart is perfect toward him. . . .

2 Chronicles 16:9

God is looking for a man, or woman, whose heart will be always set on Him, and who will trust Him for all He desires to do. God is eager to work more mightily now than He ever has through any soul. The clock of the centuries points to the eleventh hour.

"The world is waiting yet to see what God can do through a consecrated soul." Not the world alone, but God Himself is waiting for one, who will be more fully devoted to Him than any who have ever lived; who will be willing to be nothing that Christ may be all; who will grasp God's own purposes; and taking His humility and His faith, His love and His power, will, without hindering, continue to let God do exploits.

C.H.P.

Our prayer for today:

Our hearts are far from perfect, Lord. Selfish desires so often thwart our complete devotion to You. Cleanse us and fill us with faith, trust, and a new consecration, so that our lives may be used for Your Kingdom, we pray.

March 17

> . . . O Lord, I am oppressed; undertake for me.

> Isaiah 38:14

The many troubles in your household will tend to your edification, if you strive to bear them all in gentleness, patience, and kindness. Keep this ever before you, and remember constantly that God's loving eyes are upon you amid all these little worries and vexations, watching whether you take them as He would desire. Offer up all such occasions to Him, and if sometimes you are put out, and give way to impatience, do not be discouraged, but make haste to regain your lost composure.

FRANCIS DE SALES

Our prayer for today:

Teach us to face all our difficulties with a loving, forgiving spirit, Heavenly Father. We sometimes allow problems to overwhelm us, when we should be looking to You for strength to overcome.

March 18

> . . . Except a corn of wheat fall into the ground and die, it abideth alone: but if it die, it bringeth forth much fruit.

> John 12:24

"If it die. . . ." What is this death? It is the cracking open of the shell by the working of temperature and humidity, so that the true life within the grain can express itself. It is all too possible for a Christian to have the Lord's life in him and yet for that life to be confined and suppressed by the hard shell of nature. So we have the sad fact of a fruitless Christian. In this case it is not a matter of obtaining life, for that came at conversion, but of the release of that life so that it can grow and be fruitful.

WATCHMAN NEE

Our prayer for today:

Lord Jesus Christ, there is so much in our lives that needs to die so that we may be used to our utmost potential for You. By Your Holy Spirit, we ask You to break through the hardness of our hearts.

March 19

There is no fear in love; but perfect love casts out fear. . . .

1 John 4:18 NAS

Do you really believe that God loves you? In loving us, God is willing our *highest* good. He won't allow us to undergo anything that He has not *permitted* to take place for a reason. Often, God sees that our growth as Christians requires some pruning. Perfected love recognizes God's wonderful intent even as trials and hard times are upon us. Allow God's rich, flowing love to dissolve the fears that arise from time to time. Rejoice in Him, for He is perfecting us according to His will. His love isn't earned; it's unconditional. By nurturing fear in our lives, we're doubting God's motive and intentions. Fear not! Receive His perfect love.

PAT BOONE

Our prayer for today:

Our Father, whatever comes into our lives, we are comforted by the knowledge of Your perfect love for us. We ask You to forgive our needless fears and help us remember Your presence is always with us.

March 20

I am the vine, ye are the branches: He that abideth in me, and I in him, the same bringeth forth much fruit: for without me ye can do nothing.

John 15:5

Devotion is not a passing emotion—it is a fixed, enduring habit of mind, permeating the whole life, and shaping every action. It rests upon a conviction that God is the Sole Source of Holiness, and that our part is to lean upon Him and be absolutely guided and governed by Him; and it necessitates an abiding hold on Him, a perpetual habit of listening for His Voice within the heart, as of readiness to obey the dictates of that Voice.

J.N. GROU 1731–1803
French theologian

Our prayer for today:

May we lean on You, our Father, and live our lives completely devoted to You. Help us to obey Your will as You guide us each day.

March 21

. . . so that they are without excuse: Because that, when they knew God, they glorified him not as God, neither were thankful. . . .

Romans 1:20, 21

One of the basic sins of mankind, theologically, is thanklessness. The antidote is faith—a joyful thanks to God for His love for us, shown to us by Jesus Christ. Psychologically, in personal relationships, the same principle holds true. Thanklessness is the major destructive force in human relationships. "Love makes the world go 'round," the song tells us. That's only half true. It's love that starts our world going 'round, but it's thankfulness that keeps our heads spinning. The most wildly spinning romance will eventually slow down and grind to a stop if there is not a day by day thankfulness expressed in smiles, kisses, and kind words of appreciation.

CONSTANCE P. THARP

Our prayer for today:

Lord Jesus Christ, give us thankful hearts, we pray, so that we may love and praise You for Your goodness. May we show each other our love and appreciation by reaching out in tenderness.

March 22

> For it was the Father's good pleasure for all the fulness to dwell in Him. And through Him to reconcile all things to Himself, having made peace through the blood of His cross; through Him, I say, whether things on earth or things in heaven.
>
> Colossians 1:19, 20 NAS

The shadow of the Cross fell over every detail of the Life of Christ from the beginning. It fell across His Crib. His Baptism was not just a call to teach, but to be the Victim prophesied by Isaiah; it was the whole burden of Satan's temptation on the Mount; it was hinted in the cleansing of the Temple when He challenged His enemies to destroy the Temple of His Body on Good Friday and He would rebuild it on Easter; it was hidden in the title of "Savior" He accepted when He forgave a prostitute's sins; it was implied in the Beatitudes, for anyone who would practice the Beatitudes in this world would be crucified; it was prophesied clearly three times as He gave details of His Death and Resurrection; it was hidden in the seven times He used the word "Hour" in contrast to "Day" which stood for His conquest of evil.

Finally, the Cross met its defeat when the earth received its most serious wound—the empty Tomb. To create the world cost God nothing: to save it from sin cost His Life-Blood.

FULTON J. SHEEN

Our prayer for today:

The cost, the pain, the suffering—for our sakes—humbles us, Lord Jesus. Your Resurrection fills our hearts with joy!

March 23

> Blessed are the poor in spirit: for their's is the kingdom of heaven.
>
> Matthew 5:3

If "blessed are the poor in spirit" means anything at all, it means that all of my claims to spiritual achievement are disallowed, and I am left at the cross. Self-sufficiency, complacency, pride of life, condescension, class consciousness, church standing—these are the final items on the inventory to be discarded at The Place of the Skull.

Crucifixion is not a way of self-realization, but of self-sacrifice. It is the way not to spiritual riches but to spiritual poverty, not to spiritual growth but to spiritual shrinkage. It turns out not spiritual giants but spiritual pygmies.

It is only when we let go of the rope that we discover that underneath are the everlasting arms. It is only when we have no spirit left at all that we receive the filling of the Holy Spirit.

SHERWOOD ELIOT WIRT

Our prayer for today:

Our Lord, we take all our pride, all the achievements we are so delighted to brag about, and place them at the foot of Your Cross. Empty our lives of self, so that Your Holy Spirit may fill them.

March 24

For God so loved the world. . . .

John 3:16

In friendships, in parenthood, in marriage, in family relationships, in neighboring, there is the risk of hurt. . . .

The reason we can dare to risk loving others is that "God has for Christ's sake loved us." Think of it! We are loved—eternally, totally, individually, unreservedly—loved! Nothing can take God's love away. We don't have to be afraid of losing it, offending it. We don't have to earn it. We only need to accept it. We are loved. By the One who knows us best. God knows everything there is to know about us—yet He loves us. If we are so loved, we can dare to like ourselves. We don't have to be defensive or self-protective or wary. No man can do us internal harm. No rejection can discourage us. No betrayal can dishearten us. No assault can destroy us. We are loved!

GLORIA GAITHER

Our prayer for today:

Almighty God, we thank You for Your love, which can never be taken away from us. May this knowledge *really* infiltrate our lives.

March 25

And if you leave God's paths and go astray, you will hear a Voice behind you say, "No, this is the way; walk here."

Isaiah 30:21 LB

God is anxious to make His will known to you, but He rarely does so in a spectacular way. Usually, He quietly permeates your thoughts with His thoughts and patiently fills your spirit with His Spirit so that naturally, and almost spontaneously, you just know that you know what His will is. In a Christian marriage God has two channels to work through. As the marriage expands and other members become Spirit-filled Christians too, God will seek to permeate the thinking and fill the spirit of all of you so the decisions affecting all of you can be made without undue difficulty or dissension.

JOHN ALLAN LAVENDER

Our prayer for today:

Our Father, may we be sensitive to Your leading. How easy it is to blindly go our own way, when Yours is the one that brings true happiness.

March 26

No temptation has overtaken you that is not common to man. God is faithful, and he will not let you be tempted beyond your strength,

but with the temptation will also provide the way of escape, that
you may be able to endure it.

1 Corinthians 10:13 RSV

I remember the first time, many years ago, when the full impact
of that verse hit me. God was so aware of what I was to go through,
He had provided "the way of escape" even before the temptation began.

Jesus, too, was tempted—and angels ministered to Him. *Angel*
means "messenger" and those special messengers of His Spirit, along
with His earthly children whom He sends to help, will be provided
when temptation comes.

—B.B.

Our prayer for today:

Almighty God, thank You for giving us a "way of escape" from
temptation. With Your strength, we are able to bear it.

March 27

In Christ there is all of God in a human body; so you have everything when you have Christ, and you are filled with God through
your union with Christ. He is the highest Ruler, with authority
over every other power.

Colossians 2:9, 10 LB

Just this morning, as I was reading Corinthians, one verse jumped
out at me. It said,

"You know how full of love and kindness our Lord Jesus was: though
he was so very rich, yet to help you he became so very poor, so
that by being poor he could make you rich." (2 Corinthians 8:9,
LB)

How rich He was! Yet He gave it up, and through His sacrifice, we
were made rich!

It's time you woke up each morning realizing—it's time you knew it and acted on it, especially if things are going all wrong for you. It's so true—you do have everything when you have Him!

JOYCE LANDORF

Our prayer for today:

We are rich because of all Your blessings, Lord! Help us to remember this each day, as we go out into a hostile, unbelieving world.

March 28

. . . heirs together of the grace of life. . . .

1 Peter 3:7

True love involves responsibility—the one for the other and both before God. Where love is, you no longer say "I," but "you": "I am responsible for you. You are responsible for me." Together then you stand before God where you do not say "you and I," but rather "we."

Only in marriage does this "we" become a full reality. Only in marriage can love really unfold and mature, because only there can it find permanence and faithfulness. True love never can and never will end.

WALTER TROBISCH

Our prayer for today:

Lord, teach us true love. May we learn together to grow in the sanctity and beauty of Christian marriage. We praise You that we *are* "heirs together" of Your eternal life and love!

March 29

And Jesus said unto them, I am the bread of life: he that cometh to me shall never hunger; and he that believeth on me shall never thirst.

John 6:35

To feed on Christ is to get His strength into us to be our strength. You feed on the corn, and then go and build your house; and it is the corn in your strong arm that builds the house, that piles the stone and lifts the roof into place. You feed on Christ, and then go and live your life; and it is Christ in you that lives your life; that helps the poor, that tells the truth, that fights the battle, and that wins the crown.

But what is this strength of Christ that comes to us? It is His character, His strength, His purity, His truth, His mercifulness—in a word, His holiness, the perfectness of His moral life.

PHILLIPS BROOKS

Our prayer for today:

Lord Jesus, how we need Your strength in our lives! The pressures around us make it easy to fail—morally and spiritually. Help us to rely completely on You, Lord—always.

March 30

And he that believeth on him shall not be put to shame.

1 Peter 2:6 PHILLIPS

In his cross the Lord Jesus bore all our shame. The Bible records that the soldiers took the garments of Jesus off him, so that he was nearly naked when he was crucified. This is one of the shames of the cross. Sin takes our radiant garment away and renders us naked. Our Lord was stripped bare before Pilate and again on Calvary.

How would his holy soul react to such abuse? Would it not insult his sensitive nature and cover him with shame? Because every man had enjoyed the apparent glory of sin, so the Savior must endure its real indignity. Such was his love for us that he "endured the cross, despising the shame," and since he did so, whoever believes in him will never be put to shame.

WATCHMAN NEE

Our prayer for today:

The shame You suffered for our sin, Lord Jesus, overwhelms our hearts. May we live in such a way that we will glorify You, remembering Your endurance on the Cross.

March 31

> . . . his compassions fail not. They are new every morning. . . .
>
> Lamentations 3:22, 23

When Jesus told His disciples, "Therefore do not be anxious about tomorrow, for tomorrow will be anxious for itself," He was saying, "Don't try to carry today's burden *and* tomorrow's burden at the same time."

One evening a man stepped into the kitchen to help his wife with the dishes. As he was working, he thought, "If that poor woman could just look ahead and see the dishes that remain to be washed in the future, towering like a mountain ahead of her, she would give up right now!" Then he laughed. "But she only has to wash tonight's dishes, and she can handle that."

. . . No man sinks under the burden of the day. It is only when yesterday's guilt is added to tomorrow's anxiety that our legs buckle and our backs break. It is delightfully easy to live one day at a time!

CORRIE TEN BOOM

Our prayer for today:

Thank You, Lord, that You will provide us the strength and grace to live this day. May we not be anxious for the future, knowing You will be there, too!

APRIL

April 1

. . . Know what his Word says and means. Steer clear of foolish discussions which lead people into the sin of anger with each other.

2 Timothy 2:15, 16 LB

When you are in the company of unbelievers, be careful how you use the word of God. Do not cheapen it by introducing it at an inappropriate moment, when it may lead to ridicule or blasphemy.

It may be that sometimes you will need to correct someone who is in the wrong. If so, be scrupulously fair, keep calm and controlled, and do not allow yourself to be resentful or arrogant towards the person involved.

Be clear in your own mind about what you will and will not do. He who hesitates is lost!

God's name is holy—do not cheapen it. Life is precious—do not cheapen that, either—whether it be the life of the unborn child, or of a fully formed man or woman. God's gifts, like his name, should be reverenced.

Epistle of Barnabas (*c.* A.D. 120)
Paraphrased by
DAVID WINTER

Our prayer for today:

Father, let us look to You for wisdom as we meet those who do not believe in You, our Lord and God. Keep us in the power of the Holy Spirit, so we will not fail to reverence Your Holy name.

April 2

> . . . Eli, Eli, lama sabachthani? that is to say, My God, my God,
> why hast thou forsaken me?
>
> Matthew 27:46

No one knew the depths of personal suffering more than Jesus. His words from the Cross . . . will always send a chilly shudder through you. You realize that He had to drain the cup of suffering, not just take sips as you and I do.

In His suffering, however, Jesus prayed. The words, "My God, my God, why hast thou forsaken me?" are actually a form of praying. The prayer has a grim, tell-it-like-it-is honesty. Like the prayers of Job and Jeremiah, who were among God's closest companions, the prayer even arraigns God.

Jesus' prayer, "My God, why . . . ?" may be a cue for starters in your praying when you suffer. God understands your aching loneliness, and you may open the conversation with Him with the bluntness and anger which you undoubtedly feel. You may ask, "Why am I suffering?" God knows, however, that you really don't require answers. You need comfort. And He has already sent the Comforter. Your most profound needs in your suffering have already been met, but you must pray. Then keep praying.

WILLIAM P. BARKER

Our prayer for today:

Lord God, in times of suffering, questions and doubts come into our hearts. Do You hear our prayers; do You really care? Thank You for Jesus' words on the Cross. His question was answered in the Resurrection. We, too, will find answers, as we keep on praying and trusting.

April 3

> Dear Father . . . all things are possible to you. Let me not have to
> drink this cup! Yet it is not what I want but what you want.
>
> Mark 14:36 PHILLIPS

Even at the moment when Christ was bowing to the possibility of an awful death by crucifixion, He never forgot either the presence or the power of God. There is a crucial difference here between acceptance and resignation. There is no resignation in the Prayer of Relinquishment. Resignation says, "This is my situation, and I resign myself and settle down to it." Resignation lies down in the dust of a godless universe and steels itself for the worst.

Acceptance says, "True, this is my situation at the moment. I'll look unblinkingly at the reality of it. But I'll also open my hands to accept willingly whatever a loving Father sends." Thus acceptance never slams the door on hope.

Yet even while it hopes, our relinquishment must be the real thing —and this giving up of self-will is the hardest thing we human beings are ever called on to do.

CATHERINE MARSHALL

Our prayer for today:

Help us never to forget Your presence, Lord God. Teach us to accept Your will completely in our lives—with no air of resignation, but with joy.

April 4

> Jesus saith unto her, Mary. She turneth herself, and saith unto him, Rabboni; which is to say, Master.

> John 20:16

There are some sorrows that no one else can share. Mary found it so, and stood weeping at the door of the empty tomb. If we feel that we have something to cry about, how much more had she, for she could not find her Lord. In coming to the grave she only expected to find a corpse, but now even that was gone.

What was it that dried her tears and banished all her sorrows? What happened? It was just a voice saying "Mary," but it was his voice and it was her name. After that, nothing seemed to matter. So with us. When we come to an impasse from which there seems no deliverance, we only have to hear the Lord's voice speaking our name, and all is well. There is nothing more to do than to kneel down and worship him.

WATCHMAN NEE

Our prayer for today:

You know our names, Lord. The hairs of our heads are numbered. We know You love and care for us. This knowledge comforts us, and we thank You, Lord Jesus, that in times of sorrow, You are there. We are not alone.

April 5

And I will pray the Father, and he shall give you another Comforter, that he may abide with you for ever.

John 14:16

Jesus came that men and women may now begin to live—and live to Him and for Him who died and rose again for them. The resurrection was a seal that He had accomplished a mighty work for you and me. Our liberation was sealed with His own blood. It was witnessed when He rose from the dead, and it was made actual when the Holy Spirit came down on the day of Pentecost. Glorious! What did the Spirit come to give? Some people think He came to give certain spiritual gifts. Those are too small. They are part of the blessing, but they are too small to meet the whole crying need in life. He came to bring the risen Lord, the One who died, and to enthrone Him in the heart of the believer, so that the heart which was in darkness is flooded with light, and flooded with liberty, because the Liberator is inside.

FESTO KIVENGERE

Our prayer for today:

Our Lord, through Your Resurrection we are liberated! Your living presence in our hearts is proof. May we both live in such a way that those who are still imprisoned with doubt and uncertainty will be drawn to You, our living Lord and Savior.

April 6

> And if I go and prepare a place for you, I will come again, and
> receive you unto myself; that where I am, there ye may be also.
>
> John 14:3

Heaven! Our finite minds cannot comprehend all that Jesus Christ
has prepared for those who love Him. Not only will we be restored with
those loved ones in Christ who have gone before us, but—and this is
almost too wonderful to comprehend—we shall see our Lord Jesus
face-to-face!

As the minister intoned the words, "'til death do us part" at our
marriage ceremony, it seemed to me that there was a very final ring to
this phrase. Death somehow became more real to me, as I thought of
the separation it would bring, the end of our lives together on this earth.
But the mercy and love of Jesus Christ is so incredible. We know that
whoever dies first in Him will be waiting for the other one. We will live
together spiritually for all eternity.

—J.W.B.

Our prayer for today:

Thank You, Lord Jesus, for the comfort we share, knowing that You
have prepared a place for us in heaven. May our lives together here on
this earth be worthy of this great promise.

April 7

> . . . when we love each other God lives in us and his love within
> us grows ever stronger.
>
> 1 John 4:12 LB

It requires moral strength to admit to being wrong and to ask for
forgiveness. It requires even more strength to apologize, forgive, and
verbalize continuing love when you are perhaps not wrong. Remember
that forgiving also means forgetting. If God can forget, so can we.
". . . For I will forgive their iniquity, and I will remember their sin

no more" (Jeremiah 31:34).

Ask God for the gift of love for each other Many couples who come to see me no longer love each other. I help them understand each other better, to communicate better, and to work out some compromises for their differences. I point out, however, that the same God who gave them their first love can restore it if they both want it. They should then think of fresh, creative ways of expressing their newfound love.

O. QUENTIN HYDER

Our prayer for today:

Our Father, may our love rise above the pettiness of everyday pressures and be built upon the sanctity of Your forgiving, restorative love.

April 8

> And when he had sent the multitudes away, he went up into a mountain apart to pray: and when the evening was come, he was there alone.
>
> Matthew 14:23

But however many we are to get to know in a deep personal way in a lifetime, we have a need, a responsibility, and a command to spend time alone in marriage. We are to be one physically—that takes time *alone!* We are to have our physical oneness continue to be a reality in the same regular way our eating is to continue. . . . It takes time to be imaginative through years of married life in the area of physical oneness, and that means time *alone.* It takes time to be one intellectually, as it means some amount of conversation, some sharing of reading books, listening to lectures, and discussing. To grow together intellectually takes time alone. It takes time alone to grow together as one spiritually. It takes time reading the Bible together, praying together, and whatever else you arrange. Over a period of a lifetime of marriage, there have to be some *alone* periods for spiritual growth together.

EDITH SCHAEFFER

Our prayer for today:

Lord, help us to take time to be alone with each other, so that our marriage will grow. Thank You for the wonder of those moments.

April 9

. . . It is finished. . . .

John 19:30

Consider the ministry of our Lord here on earth. In the eyes of the world the cross was the ultimate in failure, and Jesus' whole life was a wasted effort. But in the eyes of heaven what appeared to be failure was the greatest success this world has ever known. Why was this so? Because Christ was in control of the whole situation. . . .

John 19:30, speaking of the death of Christ, reads: "When Jesus therefore had received the vinegar, he said, It is finished: and he bowed his head, and gave up the ghost." The phrase *he bowed his head* actually means a deliberate putting of the head into a position of rest. True, he suffered and bled and died, and in his humanity every agony was intensified. But he was not only the Son of God, he was God the Son, and as such he was in control.

JOHN HUNTER

Our prayer for today:

Jesus, in the depths of any failures we may experience, we will take comfort in You, our Savior. On the Cross, You experienced seemingly irreparable failure; yet it became a magnificent success!

April 10

For since he himself has now been through suffering and temptation, he knows what it is like when we suffer and are tempted, and he is wonderfully able to help us.

Hebrews 2:18 LB

Perhaps a problem arose between you and your partner today: Both of you took sides, and it caused a temporary separation. It might have been over money, or it just might have been a lack of communication. Perhaps the demands of marriage make you tired all the time or cause pain that you feel no one understands. Though Jesus was never married, He can relate to your problems.

Jesus understands lack of wealth. His delivery room was a stable. His occupation was that of a lowly, underpaid carpenter. During His ministry, the Bible tells us He had nowhere to lay His head.

Jesus understands separation and loneliness. His disciples forsook Him and fled. In His death, He died alone, with His Heavenly Father turning away from Him.

Jesus understands tiredness. We're told in the Scriptures that He became "wearied." On one occasion, He was so tired He slept on a boat during a violent storm.

Jesus understands suffering and pain. Even before bearing the pain of the Cross, He suffered indescribable physical and mental anguish as He was ridiculed, whipped, and crowned with thorns.

Herbert Lockyer has said, "The Christ who had never known suffering would not be the Christ for broken hearts." Because He's been there, He cares. And in caring, He offers the comfort needed to ease the ache that is trying to defeat you.

—B.B

Our prayer for today:

Our Lord Jesus, we praise You for Your love and concern for us. As we experience suffering, Lord, we thank You that we can come to You in prayer and know You understand our deepest longings and needs.

April 11

> . . . The kingdoms of this world are become the kingdoms of our Lord, and of his Christ; and he shall reign for ever and ever.
>
> Revelation 11:15

On which side of Easter are you living? Are you on the dark, dreary, defeated side, where the powers of evil still reign and death still has the final word? Or are you living on the blessed, beautiful side of the resurrection, with an assurance that Christ has won, death has been defeated, and eternal life has begun in a way that no mere cessation of physical life can hinder?

Jesus Christ said, "I am the resurrection and the life: he who lives and believes in me shall never die." But he followed this profound statement with a penetrating question: "Do you believe this?" (John 11:25).

What difference does the fact of Christ's resurrection mean to you? Has it changed your attitude about death? About the kind of life you live and the hopes you cherish?

LLOYD JOHN OGILVIE

Our prayer for today:

Our Father, because of the Resurrection of Your Son, Jesus Christ, we do not fear death. Thank You for the assurance of eternal life. Our hope is in You, our Lord and God.

April 12

> And I will pray the Father, and he shall give you another Comforter, that He may abide with you for ever.
>
> John 14:16

In a very remote part of the world, a missionary found the answer to being able to cope in a time of great crisis. Her husband had left on a tour of the bush, and shortly afterwards her child contracted polio. It was a desperate situation. Tired and alone, she knew that God understood her needs, so she kept repeating one simple sentence: "For this, I have Jesus." She was comforted and sustained.

The person of Jesus Christ is able to bring a solace to the soul that no one else can give: a peace, that tells you all will be well one day, though your heart may ache today. The Resurrection of Christ gives us hope, for we know as Christians that He is *alive* and with us.

Each day can be filled with the joy of the Resurrection, if Jesus Christ is really living in our hearts. Saint Augustine's words ring with a triumphant note amid the darkness of the world about us: "And He departed from our sight that we might return to our hearts and there find Him. For He departed, and behold, He is here!"

—J.W.B.

Our prayer for today:

May our day be filled with Your triumph, Lord, as we realize that the same power that raised You from the dead is available to us as we face whatever will come to pass, this day and always.

April 13

> Peace I leave with you, my peace I give unto you: not as the world giveth, give I unto you. . . .
>
> John 14:27

Dale worked with God to bring me something I had longed for all my life. Peace. Materially speaking, for years I had nothing. Then for years I had much. But I soon learned that having too much is worse than having too little. Nothing ever seemed quite right. I was restless, confused, unsatisfied. But the power of prayer, and the feeling of spiritual blessedness, and the love of Jesus have no price tags.

ROY ROGERS

Our prayer for today:

Lord Jesus Christ, nothing can compare with the blessing of Your peace and love in our lives. May material possessions never hinder our close relationship with You, Lord.

April 14

> . . . first cast out the beam out of thine own eye. . . .
>
> Matthew 7:5

The first question for any of us when we are in a marital storm should be "What's wrong with me? What are my faults?"

This approach may seem strange to you. For after all, your partner is 95 percent of the problem. Yet even if you are only 5 percent of the problem, the key to improvement lies with you.

Jesus said, "First, cast out the beam out of your own eye."

What are the mechanics for doing this? I suggest that you get alone with God. Simply ask, "Lord, what's wrong with me? What are my sins?" Get your pencil and paper ready, for that is a prayer God will answer.

GARY CHAPMAN

Our prayer for today:

It is hard to admit, Lord, that each of us is to blame when there are misunderstandings or unloving attitudes. We would be honest, so we come to You, asking in Jesus' name that You show us our sins.

April 15

Grow in grace. . . .

2 Peter 3:18

We err if we think that we have arrived or can arrive at the pinnacle of love in our lifetime. We grow in the grace of love until we reach heaven and are made perfect. You can water, feed and protect the apple tree from disease, insects and adverse weather. This will aid the process and affect the ultimate product. None of these efforts, however, will produce an overnight apple. So allow God to feed, water and protect you through His Word and His Spirit; but don't be impatient with either Him or yourself in your growing process.

PAMELA HEIM

Our prayer for today:

How much we have to learn of Your love, Lord! May we grow daily, as You nourish us through Your Word and Holy Spirit.

April 16

> And when they were come to the place, which is called Calvary,
> there they crucified him. . . .

> Luke 23:33

Jesus' prayer in the Garden of Gethsemane, I came to see, is the pattern for us. Christ could have avoided the Cross. He did not have to go up to Jerusalem the last time. He could have compromised with the priests, bargained with Caiaphas. He could have capitalized on His following and appeased Judas by setting up the beginning of an earthly Kingdom. Pilate wanted to release Him, all but begged Him to say the right words that would let him do so. Even in the Garden on the night of the betrayal, He had plenty of time and opportunity to flee. Instead Christ used His free will to turn the decision over to His Father.

The Phillips translation of the Gospels brings Jesus' prayer into special focus: "Dear Father . . . all things are possible to you. Let me not have to drink this cup! Yet it is not what I want but what you want" Mark 14:36 (PHILLIPS).

The prayer was not answered as the human Jesus wished. Yet power has been flowing from His Cross ever since.

CATHERINE MARSHALL

Our prayer for today:

Lord Jesus, help us to be completely surrendered to Your will for our lives. The reality of Your struggle in Gethsemane floods our hearts and gives us hope!

April 17

> And the people stood beholding. . . . saying, He saved others; let
> him save himself. . . .

> Luke 23:35

More than nineteen hundred years have passed. . . . The Cross itself has long since crumbled into dust. Yet, it stands again when we choose our own Calvary and crucify Him all over again, with every sin of commission and omission.

> Every wrong attitude . . .
> every bad disposition . . .
> every unkind word . . .
> every impure imagination . . .
> every ignoble desire . . .
> every unworthy ambition . . .

Yes, Calvary still stands, and the crowd at the top of the hill.

Were you there when they crucified my Lord? I was. . . . Were you?

PETER MARSHALL

Our prayer for today:

We examine our hearts, Lord Jesus, and find so many of the sins that crucified You. Forgive us, Lord.

April 18

My God, my God, why have you forsaken me? . . .

Psalms 22:1 LB

The words, "My God, my God, why hast thou forsaken me," which Jesus spoke from the Cross are actually a quotation from Psalm 22. If you read Psalm 22, you will be struck with the similarities between what Jesus was enduring on the Cross and what the Psalm describes. Psalm 22 is a commentary on the agonies and disgrace a crucified person would have experienced The psalm does not end, however, on a somber note of defeat. Instead, there is a triumphant shout of praise. The psalmist affirms, "Dominion belongs to the Lord, and he rules over the nations" (Psalms 22:28).

WILLIAM P. BARKER

Our prayer for today:

Our Lord, we are humbled by the knowledge of Your great suffering for us. In times of heartache, we know that our Savior cares, loves, and understands. Thank You, Lord Jesus.

April 19

> . . . Death is swallowed up in victory. O death, where is thy sting?
> O grave, where is thy victory?
>
> 1 Corinthians 15:54, 55

The glorious fact that the empty tomb proclaims to us is that life for us does not stop when death comes.

Death is not a wall, but a door.

An eternal life which may be ours now, by faith in Christ, is not interrupted when the soul leaves the body, for we live on . . . and on.

There is no death to those who have entered into fellowship with Him who emerged from the tomb.

Because the Resurrection is true, it is the most significant thing in our world to-day. Bringing the Resurrected Christ into our lives, individual and national, is the only hope we have for making a better world.

"Because I live, ye shall live also."

This is the message of Easter.

PETER MARSHALL

Our prayer for today:

Our hearts rejoice, Lord Jesus, for Your Resurrection gives us hope and comfort. When we go through the door of death, we shall live forever with You!

April 20

> [Jesus says:] Do not judge. . . . For in the same way you judge others, you will be judged. . . .
>
> Matthew 7:1, 2 NIV

Anytime you or I pray for someone else's sin or fault or hindrance, we should first pray for eyes to see our own sin or fault or hindrance. We need to be really scared of rushing into the presence of God with such a request, without talking about our own weaknesses first. He who knows us inside out is not waiting for us to be perfect before we can intercede for anyone else, but He does require us to be aware of our own need to be cleansed, as we come with our requests for others. This is true in the case of anyone we are praying for, but especially for those closest to us. As a wife or a husband, a child or a parent, when we are praying about the "faults" of anyone close to us, we need to pause long enough to examine ourselves carefully and then ask for forgiveness and for greater sensitivity to our own "blind spots." The sin of someone else can be your affliction or tribulation—or mine. But the reverse is also true. We each can be, by our sin or faults—our stubbornness or insensitivities or selfishness—the affliction or tribulation of someone close to us.

EDITH SCHAEFFER

Our prayer for today:

Dear Father, help us not to be so judgmental of each other. Show us our sins of commission and omission, and give us loving, tender hearts.

April 21

So don't be anxious about tomorrow. God will take care of your tomorrow too. . . .

Matthew 6:34 LB

Why do we fear tomorrow? Why do we doubt? If we trust today for God's grace to match our need, we can leave tomorrow to Him, for ". . . sufficient unto the day is the evil thereof."

That is the principle of God's giving. He is not going to give you grace to do something tremendous tomorrow. He is going to give you grace to be extraordinary in the ordinary circumstances of today. He is not concerned about you doing anything wonderful; He is concerned about you being wonderful in everyday life. Day by day you will receive your daily bread.

ALAN REDPATH

Our prayer for today:

Thank You, Lord, for the grace You give us each day. May we never fear the future, knowing You will be there and Your grace is sufficient.

April 22

> For we are his workmanship, created in Christ Jesus unto good works, which God hath before ordained that we should walk in them.

Ephesians 2:10

Can you imagine the builder of the *Queen Mary* standing by her in dry dock as she was ready to be launched, patting her great sides and saying, "Poor boat, I am so sorry that you have to go out into that awful sea. Just think, storms will beat on you and fierce winds will blow on you!" Why, you just laugh at the thought. That great ship was built for the storm and wind. The builder is anxious to see her launched. He wants her to try the sea.

HENRIETTA MEARS

Our prayer for today:

In the storms of our lives, You, Lord, give us the strength to survive. How often we realize that, without You, our problems could so easily submerge us in a sea of self-pity. Thank You, Lord, for Your power.

April 23

> There is therefore now no condemnation to them which are in Christ Jesus. . . .

Romans 8:1

One of the inevitable things about life is that we have got to live with ourselves. What a misery it is to live with a person you despise, a person who has allowed fear to defeat him—even if it is yourself! And unaided we cannot help despising ourselves, the more we know ourselves! It is a new self made different through Christ that we need, and we can live with that new self because Christ, not we ourselves, has made him. Many people are always searching for the approval of others to counteract their disapproval of themselves. They must see themselves "in Christ." We can be independent of the approval of others only when we approve of ourselves, and we can only approve of ourselves if we have God's approval. We can do without men's approval when we are SURE we are worth something to Christ.

LESLIE D. WEATHERHEAD
Prescription for Anxiety

Our prayer for today:

Thank You, Lord, for loving us. We do not deserve this love; yet because of it, we can learn to love ourselves. You have given us hope, forgiveness, and eternal life. We praise You!

April 24

. . . you forgave me! All my guilt is gone.

Psalms 32:5 LB

Forgiveness is the genius of Christianity. No other religious belief system places it as central as the Gospel does. What else is the Cross about? God knew when He created us that we would need forgiveness. It is for *our* benefit. I have a sneaking suspicion that most Christians have the irrational idea lurking in the back of their minds that perhaps God needs to forgive us more than we need His forgiveness. It's true that He *wants* to forgive us more than we are willing to receive it, but does He *need* to give us forgiveness? When we have sinned or our conscience is bothering us, we believe that somehow He needs us to ask for forgiveness, as if He benefited in some ways from it. No, it's the other way around. God has provided forgiveness because *we* need it.

This is the only way we can deal with our consciences, whether they are healthy or not.

ARCHIBALD D. HART

Our prayer for today:

Almighty God, thank You, that we can come to You and ask forgiveness. We think today of deeds and thoughts that have kept us from enjoying a close walk with You. Cleanse us, we pray.

April 25

. . . it [love] does not hold grudges. . . .

1 Corinthians 13:5 LB

Resentments are like snowdrifts and forgiveness is the snowplow. You see, in the eyes of many people, forgiveness is simply a matter of passive acquittal. But in the Christian context, forgiveness is a snowplow—opening the road, removing barriers, permitting communication to be restored.

There are a lot of resentments that can build up in our lives in the course of a day. And the only way to put joy on your face and in your heart is to find an overwhelming love that can remove resentments and fill you with FORGIVENESS.

"I forgive you" is the language of love!

ROBERT H. SCHULLER

Our prayer for today:

Forgive us, Lord, for the animosity that blocks our true love for each other. Cleanse our hearts, so that we may experience again the joy of unconditional love.

April 26

Having eyes, see ye not? and having ears, hear ye not? . . .

Mark 8:18

How have we come to Christ today? Have we come like the Pharisees, to argue and demand a sign? Have we been aware of all the signs
God has given already? Elizabeth Barrett Browning was right,

> Earth's crammed with heaven,
> And every common bush afire with God;
> But only he who sees takes off his shoes—
> The rest sit round it and pluck blackberries.

What more can Jesus do to convince us? Nothing. It is done.
The Cross is the sign of his love. If we take him at his word and trust
him with our lives, the power of his love will transform us and make
us a sign to our generation that Christ is alive, of what life was meant
to be, and what can happen to a person who trusts him completely.

LLOYD JOHN OGILVIE

Our prayer for today:

We trust You, Lord. You are our Savior, who bled and died upon
a Cross for our sins. Such love is amazing to us! We know You are alive,
for we have felt Your presence, and our hearts rejoice in the wonder
of Your love!

April 27

> . . . for he dwelleth with you, and shall be in you.

John 14:17

The time of business does not with me differ from the time of prayer;
and in the noise and clatter of my kitchen, while several persons are at
the same time calling for different things, I possess God in as great
tranquillity as if I were upon my knees. . . . We should establish
ourselves in a sense of God's presence by continually conversing with
him.

BROTHER LAWRENCE

Our prayer for today:

Whatever we do today, Lord, may we not forget the joy of conversing with You. A silent prayer in our hearts will be heard by You, our Savior.

April 28

The love of Christ constraineth us. . . .

2 Corinthians 5:14

As I see it, there is no way for a husband to demand submission on the part of his wife without violating the command of God for him to be loving. Let the love of Christ in him have that constraining effect on a wife and he may discover that she is no longer rebellious or fearful about the idea of submitting to that kind of leadership in the home.

"You wives must submit to your husband's leadership in the same way you submit to the Lord." There is no suggestion here that a woman submits to a man's leadership because he is superior or she is inferior. As I see it, the only possible reason she should submit to his leadership is because of the awful responsibilities he has in the eyes of God. When we elect a government official to a position of responsibility, we must confer on him the necessary authority to fulfill the responsibility. The same thing is true in the home. It is only because of the responsibility that the man must have the authority. However, since he cannot compel the woman to give him that authority, the only way he will ever get it is for her to confer that authority on him. The reason she should confer that authority on him is that he bears the responsibility that God has laid on his shoulders.

LANE ADAMS

Our prayer for today:

Lord Jesus, when we consider Your love for the church—Your death upon the Cross—we submit anew to You, our Lord and Savior. Lovingly, You show us our rightful position in life.

April 29

Be still, and know that I am God. . . .

Psalms 46:10

We were very weary, my wife and I. . . . For years I had devoted myself energetically to church work, where as everyone knows, one is always coming up against problems which seem trivial indeed compared with the task to be accomplished. And now, of a sudden, God was showing us his greatness, calling us out of the tangle of sterile arguments in which I had let myself be caught. During the year that followed he led us from experience to experience, to a renewing of our whole personal and professional life, calling us from ecclesiastical activity to a spiritual ministry.

We were both already Christians, but ours was not a very personal Christianity. We were so engrossed in his service that we had scarcely any time to listen to him. We have been taught to listen to him, at length, passionately and concretely. For us this dialogue has become interwoven with our dialogue together as man and wife, imparting to it its value and its richness.

PAUL TOURNIER

Our prayer for today:

In our busy lives, let us not forget to be still and listen to Your voice. Renew our spiritual lives with power, we pray.

April 30

For the wrath of God is revealed from heaven against all ungodliness and unrighteousness of men, who hold the truth in unrighteousness.

Romans 1:18

Love does not make anger wrong. There are things in life that demand our getting angry at them. Not to feel anger at them would mean we are either insensitive to evil or afraid to feel anger. We would be in a moral stupor if we failed to get angry at racial injustice and the hunger of children. We would be less than human if we failed to get angry at pain and the loss of precious things in our own lives. Jeremiah was seething when he said, "I am full of the wrath of the Lord; I am weary of holding it in" (Jeremiah 6:11). Jesus was furious with the Pharisees. And God's anger was kindled against Israel time and again, often enough to make him appear to be a very irritable God. Love does not forbid anger.

LEWIS B. SMEDES

Our prayer for today:

Take our anger, Lord, when we see injustice, hunger, and need, and use it to rectify these hurts in other people's lives.

MAY

May 1

And they overcame him by the blood of the Lamb, and by the word of their testimony; and they loved not their lives unto the death.

Revelation 12:11

Those of us who live in the comfort and security of our homes cannot begin to imagine what the life of a missionary is like. Many of them have no fresh water and only simple food. They constantly face the threat of sickness and infection. Some live in primitive places where their very lives are in danger. Much to my sadness, yet to the glory of God, the list is growing longer each day of men and women who are literally laying down their lives for Jesus' sake on the mission field. These men and women stand on the front lines, often in lonesome places, but knowing that their Master who has placed them there will also stand with them.

CORRIE TEN BOOM

Our prayer for today:

Thank You, Lord, for all Your missionaries in the world. We would ask You to bless and keep them in Your love, comforting those who are lonely and facing persecution.

May 2

> For he that is entered into his rest, he also hath ceased from his
> own works, as God did from his. Let us labour therefore to enter
> into that rest. . . .

Hebrews 4:10, 11

Contentment!
Beautiful, rare feeling.
The bitter taste of life, gone. The spirit of heaviness, the drag, the
ratrace—all disappeared. The ego no longer clamoring for its place in
the sun by trying to be the sun. The necessities of the moment reduced
to their proper perspective.
The body under subjection. The mind fixed on Jesus.
The spirit freshened by the Spirit of God, ready to accept what
comes, to mourn, to suffer, to laugh, to exult. The feeling that life is a
positive value, that tomorrow is a pleasant prospect—not by virtue of
circumstances but by the filling of the Holy Spirit.
The whole being tuned to the love of God and waiting for Jesus to
come back.

SHERWOOD ELIOT WIRT

Our prayer for today:

With great anticipation, we look for Your return, Lord. May our
bodies, minds, and souls be ready for that day when, "every knee shall
bow!"

May 3

> . . . lo, I am with you alway. . . .

Matthew 28:20

Do not look forward to the changes and chances of this life in
fear. Rather look at them with full hope that, as they arise, God,
whose you are, will deliver you out of them. He has kept you hith-

erto; do you but hold fast to His dear hand, and He will lead you safely through all things; and when you cannot stand, He will bear you in His arms.

Do not look forward to what may happen tomorrow. The same everlasting Father who cares for you today will take care of you tomorrow, and every day. Either He will shield you from suffering, or He will give you unfailing strength to bear it. Be at peace, then, put aside all anxious thoughts and imaginations.

FRANCIS DE SALES

Our prayer for today:

Lord, how often we are fearful, as we look ahead. Help us always to remember that You are with us. Your grace will sustain us this day and all the days that lie ahead.

May 4

No one can ever lay any other real foundation than that one we already have—Jesus Christ.

1 Corinthians 3:11 LB

What a wonderful word "home" is! Here are the most sacred and intimate associations of life. Here joys and sorrows are shared. Here God's faithfulness is proved and His blessing experienced. But, alas, the sanctity of all these things is so often lost and many of our homes today are in great need of spiritual rebuilding. Here's where we must begin if we mean business with God, upon the only foundation that can ever be laid—the foundation of Christ.

ALAN REDPATH

Our prayer for today:

Our home, Lord, envelops us with Your love. Thank You for its roof and walls, which shelter us each day. For all You provide, we praise You.

May 5

You don't understand now why I am doing it; some day you will.

John 13:7 LB

Take love out of the human heart and you will also be taking away most of our capacity to be hurt, but that is too high a price to pay. At times we must resign ourselves to our lack of understanding, but we find our strength in our faith that God knows and that God cares. The Psalmist put two wonderful statements together: "He healeth the broken in heart, and bindeth up their wounds. He telleth the number of stars; he calleth them all by their names" (Psalm 147:3, 4). That is, the God who watches over all the universe also cares for each of His children.

CHARLES L. ALLEN

Our prayer for today:

Father, sometimes it is so hard to understand circumstances. Sometimes we feel as if the hurt is not worth the underlying love we receive from each other. Forgive us. Your love makes ours seem so shallow, for You go on healing and loving, despite our lack of faith and caring.

May 6

A tenth of the produce of the land . . . is the Lord's. . . .

Leviticus 27:30 LB

There was a knock on the door of the hut occupied by a missionary in Africa. Answering, the missionary found one of the native boys holding a large fish in his hands.

"Reverend," the boy said, "You taught us what tithing is, so here— I've brought you my tithe."

As the missionary gratefully took the fish, he questioned the young lad. "If this is your tithe, where are the other nine fish?"

"Oh," said the boy, beaming, "they're still back in the river. I'm going back to catch them now."

If only we could find ourselves ready to give to the Lord with the same joy and trust that young boy had. The hardest thing for us to give up is our money, for it represents our time, our energy, and our talents, translated into dollars and cents.

Yet, when a husband and wife decide to invest and share their money for the glory of God, it becomes one of the greatest blessings they can experience together.

—B.B.

Our prayer for today:

Give us generous hearts, Father, that do not grudgingly give back to You that which is rightfully Yours.

May 7

> What a wonderful God we have . . . one who so wonderfully comforts and strengthens us in our hardships and trials. . . .
>
> 2 Corinthians 1:3, 4 LB

No one can really comfort anyone else unless there has been a measure of the same kind of affliction or some kind of suffering which has brought about an understanding and in which we have ourselves experienced the Lord's comfort. Our main motive should really be giving comfort to others as it has been given to us by the Lord in our times of trouble, so that His compassion is made known in a very real way in our circle of people. We are meant to make known the wonder of who He is by how we love one another and especially by our vivid expression of love in times of need. *His* compassion and love in giving comfort is to be reflected in *our* giving comfort. How else are people to know that God is all that His Word makes clear that He is?

EDITH SCHAEFFER

Our prayer for today:

Lord, how many times we have felt the grace of Your comfort. Let us never forget the solace that comes only from You. Use us to share Your compassion with others, Lord Jesus.

May 8

> The eyes of the Lord are watching over those . . . who rely upon
> his steady love. . . .
>
> Psalms 33:18 LB

. . . what every couple needs is some way to keep their focus on the
best.

Prayer can do that for you too.

Sometimes prayer is like the quiet moving of a hand to draw aside
some grasses. See? Here is a path we've never seen before.

Sometimes prayer is like a small voice calling and waiting. Anybody
in there? Anybody wanting to be discovered? Anyone looking for
me?

Then sometimes prayer is like a mighty bulldozer rolling over stub-
born obstacles. Moving boulders aside. Clearing a way.

But whatever else prayer is, prayer at its best is the great unifier!

That's how it's been for us.

So if I could wish for you . . . just one wish, this would be it: that
you might begin praying together in a way which makes sense to
you.

Why do I wish you this above every other wish?

I wish you this because I know from experience—

The more a husband and wife make friends together with God,

The greater He makes their friendship for each other.

CHARLIE W. SHEDD

Our prayer for today:

Our Lord, as we pray together, let the realization of Your friendship
for us become more real, more amazing! Then we shall be real friends
to each other, as we unify our hearts with You.

May 9

> Let thy fountain be blessed: and rejoice with the wife of thy youth.
>
> Proverbs 5:18

The whole book of the Song of Solomon is a love poem between two people who are in love with one another. The Bible uses very intimate and beautiful language to describe the relationship these two lovers had (*see* 1:13; 4:5, 10; 5:4, 16).

If we have background cobwebs remaining in our minds, let us ask God for the clean purifying sweep of His Word, that we may know that not only is sex within marriage straight from the hand of God, but He gave it to us a gift to *enjoy*.

JACK and CAROLE MAYHALL

Our prayer for today:

Release us, Lord, from any bonds of the past, so that we may enjoy all You intend our intimate lives together to be.

May 10

> O God, thou art my God; early will I seek thee; my soul thirsteth for thee, my flesh longeth for thee in a dry and thirsty land, where no water is; To see thy power and thy glory. . . .
>
> Psalms 63:1, 2

Only those succeed in living a peaceful, victorious, happy Christian life who have learned the profound secret of daily renewal: to turn to God incessantly for a new and fresh supply of power from the realms of eternity. That most of us live a weak Christian life is due without question to the fact that this part of our prayer life is not in order. Prayer is the breath of the soul. Our breathing is a constant source of renewal to our bodies. We eat three or four times a day, but we breathe all day long, all night too. As it is impossible for us to take a breath in the morning large enough to last us until noon, so is it impossible to pray in the morning in such a way as to last us till noon. Therefore, too, the apostle says, "Pray without ceasing" (1 Thessalonians v. 17).

O. HALLESBY

Our prayer for today:

Father, thank You, that we can come to You in prayer any moment of the day or night; for You are always with us. Teach us, Lord, to be in constant communion with You, so that we may lead a triumphant Christian life.

May 11

> The good man does not escape all troubles—he has them too. But the Lord helps him in each and every one.
>
> Psalms 34:19 LB

Understand that marriage is not always a matter of romance, of moonlight and roses. Differences will come. There will be arguments. If they do not come, something is *wrong.* I remember hearing the story of a bishop who attended a dinner at which an old man got up and said that in his thirty years of marriage, he and his wife had never had an argument. The bishop got up and said, "Now there are two things to keep clear about that statement. First, that it probably isn't true; second, if it *is* true, how ghastly!" I agree with the bishop. Troubles will come in *any* marriage; I think it is a part of God's plan and testing that they come.

DALE EVANS ROGERS

Our prayer for today:

Thank You, our Father, that You have made us different—yet one! When we have to face troubles, may we look to You and learn more of Your grace and faithfulness.

May 12

> ... And as the Spirit of the Lord works within us, we become more and more like him.
>
> 2 Corinthians 3:18 LB

Adjustments are sometimes extremely hard to make, especially when we feel our identity is at stake in a marriage. I remember that shortly after our wedding, I was still trying to hang on to all the customs of my English past. A simple thing like setting a table *my way* caused tension. Bill said, increduously, "We just don't set silverware like that, here!" and he moved the offending objects around to the American position.

"If it's good enough for the Queen of England, it's good enough for me," I retorted, deliberately returning the offending objects to their *proper* place.

We laughed about the incident afterward, and over the years I bent my will to American customs. (However, even now the British Empire continues to be represented more than surreptitiously around our house!)

Minor incidents often have been allowed to erode the foundation of a marriage, and irreparable damage has been done. Asking our Lord to be the referee in times of hurt or tensions is so important. Lovingly, He shows us our faults and gives us the grace to say, "I'm sorry."

—J.W.B.

Our prayer for today:

Coming from different backgrounds, there are so many adjustments we have to make. Help us to look to You, Lord, for guidance and grace, we pray.

May 13

> . . . and they two shall be one flesh. This is a great mystery. . . .
>
> Ephesians 5:31, 32

Movies, television, novels, magazines, and billboards constantly bombard us with wrong ideas about sex. Sex is not an invention of 20th century Hollywood. It is a creation of the eternal, holy God, who also gave us definite instructions for its right expression in the relationship of marriage. Sexual union in marriage is a wonderful mystery of God. It occupies a relatively small space in the marriage. Even with young and newly married couples, the sheer amount of time spent in sexual activity is relatively small. Yet without that union the marriage is no marriage. It is like the spark plug of a car: small but essential; it sets the whole mechanism in motion.

LARRY CHRISTENSON

Our prayer for today:

Father, thank You for making us one. Thank You, too, for the gift of love we share. Keep us from the disintegrating influences that are so prevalent in our society, we pray in Jesus' name.

May 14

. . . a threefold cord is not quickly broken.

Ecclesiastes 4:12

When Jesus Christ is given His rightful place in the marriage of two people, there is a dimension added that goes beyond the love they feel for each other. The perfect marriage is a uniting of three persons—a man, a woman, and the Lord.

Have you ever met a husband and wife who seemed to live only for each other, yet when something happened to disturb that relationship, there was nowhere to turn for healing in their marriage?

Faith in Christ is the most important of all principles in the building of a happy and successful marriage. He wants to be the One to heal the hurts and heartaches that all too often separate two lovers. In submitting to Him—and to each other—a new foundation for rebuilding can be found.

Perhaps recently there was an unkind word, a thoughtless act, between you and your partner. When spoken with His love, the words, "I'm sorry" at that moment become as beautiful as the words "I love you."

—B.B.

Our prayer for today:

Lord Jesus, because of Your love for us, we are learning more and more each day what true love really is. We thank You, Lord.

May 15

> Except the Lord build the house, they labour in vain that build
> it. . . .
>
> Psalms 127:1

People have to *work* at marriages. Marriage is a continuing challenge of constantly changing relationships as we experience the tests of life.

Marriage is also a seal. Song of Songs says, "Put me like a seal over your heart . . ." (Song of Songs 8:6). A seal requires heat, which may cause the seal to melt into a sticky mess or form a permanent bond. What kind of a marriage seal depends upon who sets the seal—the King, or one of His court jesters.

God can provide energy for a tolerable marriage and zest for a dull relationship. One of the main requirements is grasping some of His basic concepts.

Whether a marriage is made in heaven depends upon God. Whether it is lived in hell depends upon us.

CAROLE CARLSON

Our prayer for today:

Lord, what a mess we would make of our marriage without You! With Your help, we will work each day to make this union a beautiful one.

May 16

> There is a kind of man who curses his father, and does not bless
> his mother.
>
> Proverbs 30:11 NAS

The surest formula for a long life, according to God's Word, is to honor our father and mother. To dishonor our parents is to do great injury to ourselves. Not only are God-ordained relationships destroyed but God's judgment will fall upon the disobedient, bitter child. Even some Christians allow sad broken relationships with those who gave them life. If you feel that you've been hurt by your parents—and you may have—forgive them. (Even if they're no longer living.) You'll experience *healing*. Honor your father and mother, for it is pleasing to the Lord.

PAT BOONE

Our prayer for today:

Almighty God, may we always honor our parents and show them the respect and love they deserve. As we grow older, we realize the sacrifices they made for us, Lord. Thank You, Father, for giving us life through them.

May 17

... tattlers also and busybodies, speaking things which they ought not.

1 Timothy 5:13

Do people come to us because they find that they can pour all the latest gossip into our ears? The sort of talk we relish indicates the kind of people we are. In the second place, we should observe what tales we most readily credit. We are mostly more gullible in one direction than in others, and the direction of our gullibility betrays our innate weakness. Are we quick to believe the slanders of talebearers? People naturally bring supply to demand. Do we show them that it is unwelcome?

But it is those who need our help who really test us. Do people find in us those to whom they can confide their real heart problems and be met with understanding and wise counsel? Are we sensitive enough, and close enough to God, for that?

WATCHMAN NEE

Our prayer for today:

Lord Jesus, help us to keep a guard on our tongues. May we never betray another's trust in us, Lord. Let others sense the confidence of Your love for them in our lives.

May 18

> Every good gift and every perfect gift is from above. . . .
>
> James 1:17

All that is good comes from God, and that includes love. If I am to love openly and unconditionally, if I am to risk pain and rejection, if I am to be a channel of authentic love, I need to be filled and enabled by God himself. Wherever there are fulfilling relationships, there is love; and wherever there is authentic love, there is God!

The reason that many of us have tried to become lovers and have failed is that we have tried to do it in our own way—without God. In fact, many of us have mistaken lust and sexual attraction for love.

PAUL A. CEDAR

Our prayer for today:

Thank You, Father, for Your gift of love! Lord, as we continue to base our marriage on Your love, let our hearts reach out to those who are so empty.

May 19

> Every branch in me that beareth not fruit he taketh away: and every branch that beareth fruit, he purgeth it, that it may bring forth more fruit.
>
> John 15:2

It is for fruit in our lives that the Husbandman cleanses the branches. Of all the fruit-bearing plants, there is none so ready to produce wild wood, and for which cleansing and pruning are so necessary, as the grape. What is it that the vinedresser cuts away with his pruning-knife? Wood—wild wood. Why cut away this wood? Because it draws away the strength and life from the vine, and hinders the flow of sap to the grape. The wood of the branch must decrease, that the fruit of the vine may increase. Even so, the child of God is a heavenly branch, and there is in us that which seems perfectly good and even legitimate, and yet draws out our interest and strength. It must be pruned, cleansed and cut away. How easy it is to let objects and cares of this world possess and overpower us.

MORROW C. GRAHAM

Our prayer for today:

Heavenly Father, cut the "wild wood" from our lives, so that we may be used more productively for You.

May 20

For I am jealous over you with godly jealousy. . . .

2 Corinthians 11:2

Competition in business or in sport is perfectly legitimate. A shop-keeper has no right to resent the success of another retailer who threatens his business, because he cannot claim a monopoly of the local trade. Again, an athlete should not become bitter or jealous when he is beaten at this own game, because he has no personal right to an undisputed victory. His professional jealousy is but wounded vanity.

Jealousy in marriage, however, is a very different matter, because marriage is a permanently exclusive relationship. Both husband and wife have solemnly vowed that, "forsaking all other," they will keep only unto their partner, so long as they both shall live. In their married life therefore each will (or should) brook no rival. If a third party intrudes into the marriage, the offended person, whether husband or wife, is right to be jealous. In such a case it is tolerance of the rival, not intolerance, which is sin.

JOHN R. W. STOTT

Our prayer for today:

Father, keep us from making each other jealous. Jealousy is such a destructive emotion. Each day, may we be conscious of our vows to You on our wedding day.

May 21

> Confess your faults one to another, and pray one for another, that
> ye may be healed. . . .

James 5:16

It is always a denial of love, and to some extent a disavowal of marriage, to begin to calculate what one says and does not say, even when it is done with the excellent motive of safeguarding one's love. It is a contradiction of the law of marriage instituted by God: "They are no more twain, but one flesh" (Matthew 19:6).

But even in the happiest marriage personal contact cannot be a permanent state, acquired once and for all. The windows of our houses have to be cleaned from time to time if the light is to penetrate. They get dirty more quickly in the town, but there is no countryside so remote or so clean that they do not gradually lose their transparency. Between man and wife too, the true dialogue has periodically to be re-established by the confession of some secret; and the higher and more sincere our ideal of marriage, the more irksome it is to admit that we have hidden something.

PAUL TOURNIER

Our prayer for today:

Lord, let the light of Your love shine in our marriage. May we be honest with each other and You, Lord Jesus.

May 22

... learning to pray in the power and strength of the Holy Spirit.

Jude 20 LB

How wonderful it is to be able to pray for each other—not only when we are together, but during the times we are apart. The miles that separate us disappear, as we realize that our Lord is with both of us. He is nearer than breathing, and our loved one is watched over by Him.

We can pray objectively for each other's needs. The time apart can be spent fruitfully. Even the ache in our hearts for an absent loved one can be used by our Lord to deepen our prayer life. As we come closer to Him, our love is purified, and when we see our husband or wife again, a new sense of appreciation, of caring, invades us. We are closer than before, because of Jesus Christ.

—J.W.B.

Our prayer for today:

Deepen our prayer life, Lord, especially when we are apart. We thank You that we can always be assured of the comfort Your Holy Spirit brings us in times of separation.

May 23

But without faith it is impossible to please him. . . .

Hebrews 11:6

It is faith that lifts us up to heaven. It is faith that saves us from the flood tide of fear. It is faith that sets us free from our prisons, extinguishes the burning fire that threatens us, feeds us when we are hungry, raises us from death and makes nobodies into somebodies.

And what is this faith?
It is believing that God is Lord of all.

That he made the earth, the sky and the seas, and everything in
   them.
That he made man in his own image.
That he gave the law to Moses and his Spirit to the prophets.
That he sent the Messiah, Jesus, into the world, to give life to those
   who were dying.
It is believing in this and being baptized in these beliefs.
This is that faith.

APHRAATES OF PERSIA (fourth century A.D.)

Paraphrased by DAVID WINTER

Our prayer for today:

   Almighty God, let our lives together be filled with a faith that is
strong and pleasing to You: a faith that weathers the many storms we
face and goes on shining in the darkness.

May 24

   I can do all things through Christ which strengtheneth me.

Philippians 4:13

   For two people to stay in love with each other they must want to.
If they really don't have a strong desire they won't be willing to sacrifice
and work at communication. The same thing is true in the Christian
life. In Matthew 5:6 Christ said, "Blessed are they which do hunger and
thirst after righteousness." Paul said, "I have not yet attained but I
press on toward the mark . . ." (*see* Philippians 3:13, 14). Here is desire.
If you no longer have this desire, frankly admit it to the Lord and ask
Him to create it in your heart again.

CURTIS C. MITCHELL

Our prayer for today:

   Lord, in everything worthwhile, there is a sacrifice. We believe our
marriage, ordained by You, *is* worthwhile. Give us Your grace and

wisdom, so we may work each day to make this union one that is loving and strong. This is the desire of our hearts, Lord Jesus.

May 25

> I . . . beseech you that ye walk worthy of the vocation wherewith ye are called, With all lowliness and meekness, with longsuffering, forbearing one another in love.
>
> Ephesians 4:1, 2

Our feelings vary from day to day. A very close friend who has one of the greatest marriages I know shared with me a feeling she had very early in their married life. One day, all of a sudden, she looked at her husband and her heart sank. Something had happened to her feelings for him. The thrill was gone. She was conscious of saying to herself, "Okay, this is it. This is the way it's going to be. I've made a commitment to God—and to my husband—and I'm going to live by that commitment, not feelings." And so she proceeded by faith to love her husband, sincerely if not with the same sense of thrill and depth of emotional feeling. It wasn't long before one day, just as suddenly as the feeling had gone, the feeling returned . . . and more! It overflowed!

COLLEEN and LOUIS EVANS, JR.

Our prayer for today:

Lord, our feelings for each other sometimes fluctuate with the demands of life. We are tired, or we are sorry for ourselves. We long for our loved one to be different. Forgive us, Lord! You brought us together, and in faith we will live and love together.

May 26

> Therefore if any man be in Christ, he is a new creature: old things
> are passed away; behold, all things are become new.

> 2 Corinthians 5:17

Life has a religious dimension and so does marriage. There is a spiritual meaning to the failure of a marriage. The failure of a marriage is falling short of God's ideal for that relationship. The whole message of the church has to do with how God feels about people who fall short of his ideal in any area of life. He loves them. And because of his own sacrifice through the death of Christ he forgives our wrongs, restores our relationships, and begins working with us where we are to rebuild our lives.

KENNETH CHAFIN

Our prayer for today:

Show us, Lord, if we are falling short of Your ideal for our marriage. Restore the love we knew and bring us a new depth of devotion, Lord Jesus.

May 27

> The thief's purpose is to steal, kill and destroy. My purpose is to
> give life in all its fullness.

> John 10:10 LB

The Playboy philosophy, like all hedonistic philosophies, is truncated —not inclusive of all of personal life. It is representative of a diminished point of view, a restricted function at best. Sexuality is reduced to *sex* —something merely physical, something functional, something used to gain a self-centered personal pleasure. In fact, all secular views—humanistic psychology included—reduce sexuality to something less than what God designed it to be in its fullness. Quite the opposite, the Christian can hold the "grand, inclusive view" of human sexuality! No apologies!

However many seem to sense the intrinsic mystery and sanctity of sex, the greater proportion of people nonetheless continue to exploit the physical pleasure as if it were something self-contained, an end in itself. They evade the responsibilities which stabilize sex, hence fail to integrate sex into the larger purposes which God has established in marriage. This, in turn, brings about a lesser fulfillment than God intends. The result is *less,* when God intends *more.*

DWIGHT HERVEY SMALL

Our prayer for today:

Father, thank You for the joy we experience together in our marriage. The fullness of our love is expressed in the gift You have given to us.

May 28

... when your body suffers, sin loses its power, and you won't be spending the rest of your life chasing after evil desires, but will be anxious to do the will of God.

1 Peter 4:1, 2 LB

The most illustrious characters of the Bible were bruised and threshed and ground into bread for the hungry. Abraham's diploma styles him as "the father of the faithful." That was because he stood at the head of his class in affliction and obedience.

Jacob suffered severe threshings and grindings. Joseph was bruised and beaten and had to go through Potiphar's kitchen and Egypt's prison to get to his throne.

David, hunted like a partridge on the mountain, bruised, weary and footsore, was ground into bread for a kingdom. Paul never could have been bread for Caesar's household if he had not endured the bruising, whippings and stonings. He was ground into fine flour for the royal family.

MRS. CHARLES E. COWMAN

Our prayer for today:

Father, whenever we are "bruised," we will remember those in the Bible who suffered and were used by You. May we be ready to do Your will, strengthened by Your Holy Spirit.

May 29

My brethren, count it all joy when ye fall into divers temptations [or *trials*]; Knowing this, that the trying of your faith worketh patience.

James 1:2, 3

We have need of patience with ourselves and with others; with those below, and those above us, and with our own equals; with those who love us and those who love us not; for the greatest things and for the least; against sudden inroads of trouble, and under our daily burdens; disappointments as to the weather, or the breaking of the heart; in the weariness of the body, or the wearing of the soul; in our own failure of duty, or others' failure toward us; in every-day wants, or in the aching of sickness or the decay of age; in disappointment, bereavement, losses, injuries, reproaches; in heaviness of the heart; or its sickness amid delayed hopes. In all these things, from childhood's little troubles to the martyr's sufferings, patience is the grace of God, whereby we endure evil for the love of God.

E.B. PUSEY

Our prayer for today:

Almighty God, we ask for Your grace to overcome the many disappointments, irritations, and heartaches that we face each day. Thank You for the assurance that Your love conquers all the evil we encounter.

May 30

> But they that wait upon the Lord shall renew their strength.
> . . .

Isaiah 40:31

You will also go through times when you will not feel very religious or when God will not seem very real or close. Your mood will not always be prayerful. You will be tempted to skip praying.

You with all the saints will also go through the "dark night of the soul" from time to time. When you experience these times when praying comes slow and hard, "Wait on the Lord: be of good courage, and he shall strengthen thine heart" (Psalms 27:14 KJV). Hang on! Refreshment is promised! Like the thirsty person who struggles across the desert and gives up just short of the oasis, you may quit too soon. Keep going: keep praying!

WILLIAM P. BARKER

Our prayer for today:

Our Father, in times of drought in our prayer life, we will keep praying, believing You are there. Forgive our fluctuating moods. Strengthen our hearts, we pray.

May 31

> But the very hairs of your head are all numbered.

Matthew 10:30

We sometimes fear to bring our troubles to God, because they must seem so small to Him who sitteth on the circle of the earth. But if they are large enough to vex and endanger our welfare, they are large enough to touch His heart of love. For love does not measure by a merchant's scales, nor with a surveyor's chain. It hath a delicacy which is unknown in any handling of material substances.

R. A. TORREY

Our prayer for today:

We remember, Lord, that You care for the minutest detail in our lives. Thank You for Your overwhelming care and concern.

JUNE

. . . but how can one be warm alone?

Ecclesiastes 4:11

I am married, I am married, and my heart is glad.

I will give thanks unto the Lord for the love and protection of my husband. I will give thanks for the blessed protection and satisfaction of my home. I will give thanks that I have someone of my own to help and comfort and even to worry about, someone to encourage and to love.

My husband is beside me wherever I need to go. My husband is behind me supporting me in whatever I need to do. I need not face the world alone. I need not face my family alone.

I need face only myself and my God alone. And this is good. This is very good.

Whatever our differences, whatever our trials, I will give thanks unto the Lord for my husband and my marriage. For so long as I have both my husband and my God I am a woman complete, I am not alone.

MARJORIE HOLMES

Our prayer for today:

Thank You, Father, for our partner's love. When differences come, help us to see what blessings we have together in You.

June 2

> Accept one another. . . .
>
> Romans 15:7 NIV

When two believers marry, they have an exciting advantage right from the beginning. They have God's standards for their relationship. The Bible is a practical book, providing us with guidelines and principles that work. . . .

God doesn't tell us that before He could love and accept us we have to change the way we keep our checkbook, the color and style of our hair, or when we eat our meals. He accepts us just as we are. The change will come as we grow in His love and seek to please Him. . . .

"Now may the God who gives perseverance and encouragement grant you to be of the same mind with one another according to Christ Jesus; that with one accord you may with one voice glorify the God and Father of our Lord Jesus Christ. Wherefore, accept one another, just as Christ also accepted us to the glory of God" (Romans 15:5-7).

Acceptance. What a wonderful concept! Most of the time we need to accept each other "in spite of" the way we are. Sometimes acceptance has to be accompanied by a sense of humor.

CAROLE C. CARLSON

Our prayer for today

Lord Jesus, sometimes our lives become so narrow, so insular, and we focus on each other's faults. Teach us to see the good in each other, not with unrealistic eyes, but with eyes that radiate Your love and understanding.

June 3

> And thou shalt love the Lord thy God with all thy heart, and with all thy soul, and with all thy mind, and with all thy strength. . . .
>
> Mark 12:30

Christian marriage is for three people: a husband, a wife, and our Lord. When two people have given their lives to the Lord, then they can give themselves to each other. The sickness of so many marriages is exposed at exactly this point. A great Christian marriage is the unrestricted giving of mind, emotion, will and soul to another, as if given to Christ. . . . When two minds are yielded to the guidance of Christ, two emotional natures are surrendered to express the love of Christ, two wills are committed to discern and do the will of Christ, two souls are galvanized to seek the Kingdom of God together, and two bodies are given freely to satisfy and enjoy each other—that's the expression of God's intention for marriage.

LLOYD JOHN OGILVIE

Our prayer for today:

Teach us to give to each other a love that is Christlike, Lord. Together may we find true freedom to express the joy You have given us. May our lives be completely surrendered to Your will.

June 4

For this cause shall a man leave his father and mother, and shall be joined unto his wife, and they two shall be one flesh. This is a great mystery. . . .

Ephesians 5:31, 32

Psalm for a Good Marriage

Lord God of Earth and Sky, whose hand hath harnessed
   the wind and the rain, whose ear hath marked the
   pounding of the surf and the small night stir of
   crickets in the grass;
Bless them this day!
Make Thy light to shine upon their faces as they cross
   the threshold of this wedded life;
Let their souls be the wide windows to the sun and
   their minds open to the light of mutual understanding;

Let contentment be as a roof over their heads and
    humility as a carpet for their feet;
Give them love's tenderness for their days of sorrow
    and love's pride for their days of joy. . . .
Make theirs in truth a good marriage—
For Ever and Ever.

AUTHOR UNKNOWN

Our prayer for today:

We remember our wedding day, Lord. It was filled with wonder and joy, as we realized You had made us one. Amid the pressures of life, may we keep that tender love for each other.

June 5

. . . being knit together in love. . . .

Colossians 2:2

Sex is a gift from God—and also a gift that husbands and wives give each other. It is the physical expression of the total commitment to each other originally pledged on a spiritual level at the wedding ceremony. It is, however, more than the gift of physical pleasure. It is the most complete way of total giving of oneself to the other. It is the most personal, intimate, and sacramental outward expression of the inner physical and spiritual love which God has given. Sexual intercourse within Christian marriage is the highest symbolic act which our mortal bodies are capable of performing, and as such represents worship and thanksgiving to the God of love who created us.

O. QUENTIN HYDER, M.D.

Our prayer for today:

Lord God, whenever we perform the physical gift of our marriage, we express our praise and thanksgiving to You, the Almighty and everlasting God.

June 6

Come now, and let us reason together, saith the Lord. . . .

Isaiah 1:18

What is the secret of maintaining a love relationship? What is the key? Almost all books on marriage come back to one basic concept as the key for two people maintaining a high-level love relationship with each other. That is *communication.* You show me a man and woman who are not communicating, and I'll show you a love relationship that is going to be in trouble. They may still stay married, but when love goes, the real heart of that relationship goes. You've got to communicate with a person to stay in love with him or her. Now the same thing is true between you and Jesus Christ. You are a person and He is a Person. If you are going to stay in love with Him, you are going to have to communicate with Him.

CURTIS C. MITCHELL

Our prayer for today:

May we love You, Lord Jesus, in such a full, glorious way that our communication will be vital and wonderful.

June 7

And the Lord God fashioned into a woman the rib which He had taken from the man, and brought her to the man.

Genesis 2:22 NAS

Since God created woman from one of the ribs of the man, woman is part of man and therefore equal to him. It is important to note that woman is not less than man, nor was she created as an afterthought. She is a vital part of God's original design. Adam had a need that God provided for through Eve. You have a need—you are alone— and God has provided for that need through your mate. You must acknowledge that your mate is God's provision for your problem of aloneness. This is not to say that you have no need for other people, but that the marital relationship is unique, completing you to a degree that no other can.

TIM TIMMONS

Our prayer for today:

Thank You, our Father, for bringing us together so that we may comfort and care for each other. May we never take for granted this gift from You.

June 8

Let love be your greatest aim. . . .

1 Corinthians 14:1 LB

Love delights in giving attention rather than in attracting it.
Love finds the element of good and builds on it.
Love does not magnify defects.
Love is a flame that warms but never burns.
Love knows how to disagree without becoming disagreeable.
Love rejoices at the success of others instead of being envious.

FATHER JAMES KELLER

Our prayer for today:

Jesus, in all our days together, we would remember Your life here on earth. Your example makes us realize how far short our finite love falls. May our eyes be ever on You, our Savior.

June 9

. . . the two become one person.

Genesis 2:24 LB

With the emphasis on sex that is fed to us daily by television, films, and newspapers, we're made to think that the highest form of communication between two people is physical. Sexual communication is made ideal only when the strength of the other levels of our relationship is blended into the physical act. Though important, sexual communication alone never held a marriage together.

Communication is a twenty-four-hour-a-day experience. It is the sharing of our minds, the opening of ourselves to each other. Communication is enjoying the other's past. It involves respecting the other's judgments. Communication means taking joy in the plans that lie ahead. Patience, forgiveness, and trust are three of its attributes.

I'm grateful to the Lord for a wife with whom it has always been easy, and a joy, to communicate. As our two minds and hearts have grown closer together in Him and each other over the past twenty-five years, our marriage has taken on a meaning that is so much deeper than when it began.

—B.B.

Our prayer for today:

Thank You, Lord, for the joy of growing together in our marriage. Help us to be always open, honest, and loving toward each other.

June 10

> I have become absolutely convinced that neither death nor life, neither messenger of Heaven nor monarch of earth, neither what happens today nor what may happen tomorrow, neither a power from on high nor a power from below, nor anything else in God's whole world has any power to separate us from the love of God in Christ Jesus our Lord!
>
> Romans 8:38, 39 PHILLIPS

So what must we do to enter into this highest relationship?

Entering into a marriage relationship is an almost perfect analogy. We want to enter into it. We make a decision. We take a definite step at the moment of the marriage ceremony.

We take that step, even though we know that a risk is involved. We cannot know what the future may hold: we cannot guess that the joys of the comradeship will outweigh the risk.

Instinctively, we feel that there is risk involved in entering into a relationship with our God. How can we know what He may require of us?

But when we guess that the joy of the relationship and having His love in our empty hearts may outweigh the risk and we take the step anyway—that is taking a step in faith.

CATHERINE MARSHALL

Our prayer for today:

Dear Lord, our decision to follow You has brought us full and beautiful days together, because we are now one in You. Keep us close to each other through Your ever-flowing love. Thank You for Your gift of marriage.

June 11

Now is my soul troubled; and what shall I say? Father, save me from this hour: but for this cause came I unto this hour.

John 12:27

At Cana, it was the joy of the nuptials that came first—the nuptials of the Bridegroom and the Bride of redeemed humanity; only after that are we reminded that the Cross is the condition of that ecstasy.

Thus He did at a marriage feast what He would not do in a desert; He worked in the full gaze of men what He had refused to do before Satan. Satan asked Him to turn stones into bread in order that He might become an economic Messiah; His mother asked Him to change water into wine that He might become a Savior. Satan tempted Him *from* death; Mary "tempted" Him *to* death and Resurrection. Satan tried to lead Him *from* the Cross; Mary sent Him *toward* it. Later on, He would take hold of the bread that Satan had said men needed, and the wine that His mother had said the wedding guests needed, and He would change them both into the memorial of His Passion and His death. Then He would ask that men renew that memorial, even "unto the consummation of the world." The antiphon of His life continues to sing: *Everyone else came into the world to live; He came into the world to die.*

FULTON J. SHEEN

Our prayer for today:

Thank You, Lord Jesus, for dying for us. As we take communion, we will remember again Your agony and Your triumph.

June 12

Love never fails. . . .

1 Corinthians 13:8 NIV

The first essential for a happy Christian home is that love must be practiced. Homes that are built on animal attraction and lust, or on anything other than love, are destined to crumble and fall. Love is the cohesive force that holds the family together. True love contains an element of spiritual mystery. It embodies loyalty, reverence, and understanding. Love imposes a tremendous responsibility on all members of a family, but it is a responsibility accompanied by glorious rewards. "Love," says the Bible, "even as Christ . . . loved the church, and gave Himself for it." How did Christ love the church? He loved it despite its faults, its mistakes, and its weaknesses. True love does not fail. It loves despite personality defects, physical blemishes, and mental quirks. Love is deep, abiding, and eternal. Nothing can bring a sense of security into the home as true love can.

BILLY GRAHAM

Our prayer for today:

May we so love each other that our faults will be superseded by this beautiful gift from You: Your love and forgiveness.

June 13

What we suffer now is nothing compared to the glory He will give us later.

Romans 8:18 LB

"With this ring . . ."
your strong, familiar voice
fell like a benediction
on my heart, that dusk;
tall candles flickered gently,
our age-old vows were said,
and I could hear
someone begin to sing
an old, old song,
timeworn and lovely,
timeworn and dear.
And in that dusk
were old, old friends—
and you,
an old friend too,
(and dearer than them all).
Only my ring seemed new—
its plain gold
surface
warm and bright
and strange to me
that candlelight . . .
unworn—unmarred.
Could it be that wedding rings
like other things,
are lovelier when scarred?

RUTH BELL GRAHAM

Our prayer for today:

Father, a look at the wedding ring is a reminder of our days together. Some have been scarred, others filled with joy and laughter. Always, they have been filled with Your presence and care. Thank You, Lord.

June 14

> But God commendeth his love toward us, in that, while we were
> yet sinners, Christ died for us.
>
> Romans 5:8

There is a story about the wife of one of Cyrus's generals who was charged with treachery against the king. She was called before Cyrus and after the trials condemned to die.

Her husband, who did not realize what had taken place, was apprised of it and came hurrying in. When he heard the sentence condemning his wife to death, he threw himself prostrate before the king and said, "Oh, Sire, take my life instead of hers. Let me die in her place!" Cyrus was so touched that he said, "Love like that must not be spoiled by death," and he gave them back to each other and let the wife go free.

As they walked happily away the husband said, "Did you notice how kindly the king looked upon us when he gave you a free pardon?"

"I had no eyes for the king," she said. "I saw only the man who was willing to die for me."

H. A. IRONSIDE

Our prayer for today:

Lord Jesus, we think of the way in which You died an ignominious, torturous death for our sins. Such love demands our devotion. In loving You as we should, may we love each other, not counting the cost, compassionately, and tenderly.

June 15

> And the Lord said, Who then is that faithful and wise stew-
> ard . . . ?
>
> Luke 12:42

We realized, during our early years of Christian life, God did not need our money, even though He asked for it; but rather we needed the great experience of giving and sharing with God. Once we began tithing we found that God blessed our lives in three ways: We had financial wisdom—to our surprise; we had paying investments; and we had an open opportunity account which taught us to use what we had, not what we wished we had. We were to learn too that God, His church, or His ministers were not out to get our money because when God has the man, He automatically has the man's wallet. Giving, gradually becomes a trip into the miraculous.

JOYCE LANDORF

Our prayer for today:

Almighty God, from whom we receive all our needs and more, teach us to give to You from grateful and willing hearts.

June 16

But the wisdom from above is first pure, then peaceable, gentle, reasonable, full of mercy and good fruits, unwavering, without hypocrisy.

James 3:17 NAS

I believe that one of the ways that we demonstrate grace in our relationships and show that we are gracious individuals is to have the courage to share honestly with another person what the conflict means to us and how we think it should be resolved. This can only be done through prayer and with a great deal of mental rehearsing of what we want to say. Usually, we will have to come up with several alternatives before we find one that is an acceptable resolution for both parties. One of the important elements of this process is to be, as the Scripture says in James 1:19, "a ready listener." We need to listen carefully to the other person, and then, with a proper tone of voice, and having thought it out, share some possibilities and some alternatives.

H. NORMAN WRIGHT
and
REX JOHNSON

Our prayer for today:

We need Your grace when facing conflicts, Lord. So often we speak with an unloving spirit, not waiting for Your leading. May we take time to listen to You and those with whom we are in disagreement.

June 17

... Every sin that a man doeth is without the body; but he that committeth fornication sinneth against his own body.

1 Corinthians 6:18

The Christian idea of marriage is based on Christ's words that a man and wife are to be regarded as a single organism—for that is what the words "one flesh" would be in modern English. And the Christians believe that when He said this He was not expressing a sentiment but stating a fact—just as one is stating a fact when one says that a lock and its key are one mechanism, or that a violin and a bow are one musical instrument. The inventor of the human machine was telling us that its two halves, the male and the female, were made to be combined together in pairs, not simply on the sexual level, but totally combined.

C. S. LEWIS

Our prayer for today:

Our marriage is sanctified by You, Lord Jesus. Our love must be true at all times. Keep us from temptation and make us worthy of Your love and each other's.

June 18

... Yea, I have loved thee with an everlasting love: therefore with lovingkindness have I drawn thee.

Jeremiah 31:3

If ever human love was tender, and self-sacrificing, and devoted; if ever it could bear and forbear; if ever it could suffer gladly for its loved ones; if ever it was willing to pour itself out in a lavish abandonment for the comfort or pleasure of its objects; then infinitely more is Divine love tender, and self-sacrificing, and devoted, and glad to bear and forbear, and to suffer, and to lavish its best of gifts and blessings upon the objects of its love. Put together all the tenderest love you know of, the deepest you have ever felt, and the strongest that has ever been poured out upon you, and heap upon it all the love of all the loving human hearts in the world, and then multiply it by infinity, and you will begin, perhaps, to have some faint glimpse of what the love of God is.

HANNAH WHITALL SMITH

Our prayer for today:

Almighty God, our finite minds cannot even begin to grasp the magnitude of Your tender love for us. May we draw closer to You and love You as we should—from grateful, devoted hearts.

June 19

Let us search and try our ways, and turn again to the Lord.

Lamentations 3:40

. . . the other day the awning on my trailer blew away. (I often run away from telephones and tensions to do my writing in a trailer parked near a beach.) The thing just took up and off, and I thought for a minute that the whole trailer and everything in it, including me, would land in the Pacific. The wind was strong, and the man who set up the awning hadn't driven its poles deep enough into the ground, and off it went. Marriages often take off and up for the same reason: they are not grounded deeply enough in God's Word and in prayer. When the storms come, they are uprooted. This is why marriages based on a slender faith have such a slim chance of happiness, of growth, and even of plain survival.

DALE EVANS ROGERS

Our prayer for today:

Our Father, when the storms come in our marriage, let us be prepared by Your Word. May our love not be shallow, but grounded in the strength of Your divine love.

June 20

And you husbands, show the same kind of love to your wives as Christ showed to the church when he died for her. . . .

Ephesians 5:25 LB

A young fellow, who had taken to his heart and home a beautiful bride, came in distress one day and said, "Brother Ironside, I want your help. I am in an awful state. I am drifting into idolatry."

"What is the trouble?" I asked.

"Well, I am afraid that I am putting my wife on too high a plane. I am afraid I love her too much, and I am displeasing the Lord."

"Are you indeed?" I asked. "Do you love her more than Christ loved the Church?"

"I don't think I do."

"Well, that is the limit, for we read, 'Husbands, love your wives, even as Christ also loved the church, and gave himself for it.' "

You cannot get beyond that. That is a self-denying love, a love that makes one willing even to lay down his life for another.

H.A. IRONSIDE

Our prayer for today:

Your love for the church, which sent You to the excruciating agony of the Cross, humbles us, Lord Jesus. We have so much to learn of what Christlike love for each other really is. Thank You for bringing us together in the light of this amazing love.

June 21

> . . . I am come that they may have life, and that they might have
> it more abundantly.

> John 10:10

When the ceremony has ended and the last piece of cake has been eaten, the bride and groom will leave. Friends will pelt them with rice and wish them well. And these two persons who once were strangers will enter into a relationship that has been ordained by God for the benefit of man. Within the framework of this new family unit will come the children who someday will shape the culture of their time. And hopefully many will hold out the message of love that will shape the destinies of men's souls.

Marriage is both high privilege and solemn responsibility—and a call to an adventure in abundant living under the Lordship of Jesus Christ.

ANTHONY FLORIO

Our prayer for today:

Our Lord, thank You for the joy of married life. There are days when we find we are still adjusting to being one; keep our hearts flexible with Your love, Lord. We praise You for being able to share the wonder of Your abundant life!

June 22

> God is at work within you, helping you want to obey him, and then
> helping you do what he wants.

> Philippians 2:13 LB

In my own experience as a husband and father, I have to say that my wife and children have no doubts that I have the God-given responsibility to make the final decision at times. But I am so aware of my own fallibility that I never make major decisions without adequately exposing myself to the alternatives presented by family in general, and my wife in particular.

Then because someone has to make the final decision in the light of all the input from the family, I carefully do it, but in great humility because I understand the feelings of all concerned. There is no suggestion of authoritarianism or dictatorial attitude on my part. Neither is there a sense of slavery or inferiority on the part of my wife or children, only a great sense of concern for each other and responsibility to God for the decisions made and the actions taken.

In 19 years of marriage I can only remember two occasions when we have had a disagreement which necessitated my putting my manly foot down! My wife says there were three occasions and I was wrong on the first which I have conveniently forgotten and right on the two I remember!

D. STUART BRISCOE

Our prayer for today:

Lord, thank You for the gift of each other. Thank You, too, that Your Word shows us our responsibilities. Lovingly, we submit to Your authority, Lord Jesus.

June 23

> . . . we know not what we should pray for as we ought: but the Spirit itself maketh intercession for us with groanings which cannot be uttered.
>
> Romans 8:26

Oh, how God has spoken to me in my prayer times and taught me to be honest with myself, with Him, and then with those against whom I have sinned. Prayer has revealed my poverty of spirit, my bigoted attitudes toward those I am sent to serve. In prayer God has shattered the ice of my soul and set me free to love! He has answered my prayers —not as I told Him to, praise God—but with a whale of a storm, a group of difficult people, or a seemingly impossible assignment. He has listened deeper than my superficial request and answered the hidden needs of my character. He has ignored my petitions for physical ease, and yet strangely answered them by giving me rest in distress, comfort in adversity. . . .

JILL BRISCOE

Our prayer for today:

Lord Jesus, strip the facade from our lives and help us pray with complete honesty. Break through the hardness of our hearts and fill them with Your love, for we do not know how we should pray, Lord.

June 24

. . . if we love each other God does actually live within us, and his love grows in us towards perfection.

1 John 4:12 PHILLIPS

Where there is love the heart is light,
Where there is love the day is bright,
Where there is love there is a song
To help when things are going wrong . . .
Where there is love there is a smile
To make all things seem more worthwhile,
Where there is love there's quiet peace,
A tranquil place where turmoils cease—
Love changes darkness into light
And makes the heart take "wingless flight" . . .
Oh, blest are they who walk in love,
They also walk with God above—
And when you walk with God each day
And kneel together when you pray,
Your marriage will be truly blest
And God will be your daily "GUEST"—
And love that once seemed yours alone,
God gently blends into HIS OWN.

HELEN STEINER RICE

Our prayer for today:

Lord, may our daily walk with You reflect the beauty of Your love. May others see in our marriage the unity that comes from You.

June 25

. . . that house . . . it fell not: for it was founded upon a rock.

Matthew 7:25

Following our wedding, several people told Joan and me, "You two were made for each other." We took it as a compliment.

Yet, on reflection, that was a strong statement. It suggested that our personalities fit so perfectly together that we would have no big adjustments to make—an ideal marriage was guaranteed, without any effort.

Marriage just doesn't happen that way in real life. For all couples, there are difficult adjustments; there are rough roads ahead.

But for the Christian couple, the success of their marriage rests firmly on a foundation of faith in each other and in the Lord who brought them together.

A oneness of spirit and the assurance—amid all difficulties—that their marriage was formed in heaven, provide the Christian couple with a determination to work toward the future they dreamed of when they stood together at the altar.

—B.B.

Our prayer for today:

With Your guidance, our Father, may all our future plans and endeavors fall within Your will.

June 26

. . . I have loved you, O my people, with an everlasting love. . . .

Jeremiah 31:3 LB

When Bill and I were first married, I loved him selfishly. I needed him in my life not only as a husband, but as a father-figure, too. Circumstances from the past made me want to lean on him completely. I expected the impossible: a man who could fulfill all my needs. In many ways, he also required the impossible of me. The pedestals we had placed each other on cracked rather quickly —mine much faster than his! We expected from each other what only God could be to us.

Then one day I heard the late Bishop Fulton Sheen say that God is the flame of love in our lives, and we are simply the sparks of that flame. Now when I find myself frustrated in our relationship, I stop and think of whether I am expecting too much of my husband. Usually I see that my need is in an area that only God can satisfy, and I stop trying to make Bill do the impossible—take God's place.

—J.W.B.

Our prayer for today:

Father, help us stop expecting perfection from each other and trying to be what only You can be: the One who fills completely the vacuum that is meant for Your divine presence.

June 27

So husbands ought also to love their own wives as their own bodies.
He who loves his own wife loves himself.

Ephesians 5:28 NAS

We reap what we sow. If we sow seeds of love, selflessness and sacrifice in our marriage relationships, somewhere down the line, we'll be repaid in wonderful tangible ways. The marriage will be strengthened, the family will be stable and we'll enjoy benefits and blessings absolutely unavailable to the self-centered. Best of all, we'll come to know God—because the family is His training ground for heaven.

PAT BOONE

Our prayer for today:

Our Father, strengthen our marriage with the power of Your unselfish love. Take away any selfish motives we have. We ask in Jesus' name.

June 28

Forgive us . . . as we forgive. . . .

Matthew 6:12

Another great thing Christ does in a marriage is to forgive and heal. A marriage is closer to being genuinely Christian at its core not when it is free of all difficulties but when both partners are open to the work of God in their lives. There is no perfect marriage, no marriage that does not need God's forgiving ways as part of its everyday life-style. In this atmosphere two people can feel forgiven by God and so be generous in forgiving one another. In this atmosphere healing takes place, and love and growth walk hand in hand. It is a beautiful thing to see a couple allow God to release his grace and power in their lives at the very point of their need.

COLLEEN and LOUIS EVANS, JR.

Our prayer for today:

Give us Your grace, Lord, to forgive each other, we pray. So much time is lost when we allow differences to turn into insurmountable barriers between us. We need the generosity of Your love in our hearts, Lord Jesus.

June 29

But the wisdom that comes from heaven is first of all pure and full of quiet gentleness. Then it is peace-loving and courteous. It allows discussion and is willing to yield to others; it is full of mercy and good deeds. . . .

James 3:17 LB

To keep romance in marriage, husband and wife should practice mutual openness in attitudes, words, and deed. They should be able to see clearly through each other's feelings and emotions, like seeing a fish in a crystal-clear lake. To close up like a clam does not indicate depth or wisdom, but shallowness, insecurity, and fear. Husband and wife should let their feelings flow outward to each other like the music from a mockingbird, or the flashes of light from her diamond. Some couples can live together for twenty years without knowing each other. This is sad, sad indeed. They are missing the ripe fruits of romantic love. No! Love cannot be taken for granted. Love must be openly manifested. Love can be known and can grow only through free expression.

HERBERT and FERN HARRINGTON MILES

Our prayer for today:

Our Father, help us to really *know* each other. May we always be open and loving, free to grow in our lives together.

June 30

Pilate therefore said unto him, Art thou a king, then? Jesus answered, Thou sayest that I am a king. To this end was I born, and for this cause came I into the world, that I should bear witness unto the truth. . . .

John 18:37

We cry when we leave our homes to venture out into a world we long to explore. So Christ was sorrowful that the time had come when he must leave loving friends and disciples, the road to Bethany in the deepening dusk, the Lake of Galilee and the fishing boats coming in with their catches—all the familiar scenes and dear companionship he had known on earth. *O, my, Father,* he prayed, *if it be possible, let this cup pass from me: nevertheless, not as I will, but as thou wilt,* reflecting, as he must have done, how easy it would be for him to slip away by himself, back to Galilee, and a happy private life there like other men, with a wife, children and all the other mitigations of the loneliness and mystery of our human fate. How easy, and how impossible!

MALCOLM MUGGERIDGE

Our prayer for today:

Lord Jesus, how we love our home. We think of You leaving Yours for us, and we praise and thank You, our Lord and Savior.

JULY

July 1

Be kindly affectioned one to another with brotherly love. . . .

Romans 12:10

Living creatively for Christ in the home is the acid test for any Christian man or woman. It is far easier to live an excellent life among your friends, when you are putting your best foot forward and are conscious of public opinion, than it is to live for Christ in your home. Your own family circle knows whether Christ lives in you and through you. If you are a true Christian, you will not give way at home to bad temper, impatience, fault-finding, sarcasm, unkindness, suspicion, selfishness, or laziness. Instead, you will reveal through your daily life the fruit of the Spirit, which is love, joy, peace, long-suffering and all the other Christian virtues which round out a Christlike personality.

BILLY GRAHAM

Our prayer for today:

We fail each other so many times, Lord, saving our best side for our friends and acquaintances. Help us to love, honor, and cherish each other, as we promised You on our wedding day.

July 2

Then shall he say also unto them . . . Depart from me, ye cursed. . . . For I was an hungred, and ye gave me no meat. . . .

Matthew 25:41, 42

"Bread for myself is an economic problem, bread for my brother is a spiritual problem," stated Nikolai Berdyaev, the Russian philosopher. When you sit down at any meal, you never eat as the only member of God's family. The needs of your brothers and sisters are on God's mind, and must be in your prayers.

You have probably heard so much about world hunger during the past few years that you are weary and bored. Like the disciples, you feel like shrugging that you have only slender resources and ask "What are they among so many?" (John 6:9.) Jesus still commands, however, "You give them something to eat!" (Matthew 14:16.)

Therefore, pray when you eat. Pray that you may be so sensitized to the goodness and nearness of Jesus Christ that you may care. Pray that you may be so sensitized to the needs of brothers and sisters that you may share.

WILLIAM P. BARKER

Our prayer for today:

Almighty God, each time we eat, let us remember Your goodness. Burden our hearts for those who are hungry in the world—not only for bread, but for You. May this burden become one of action, Lord.

July 3

This I declare, that he alone is my refuge, my place of safety; he is my God, and I am trusting him.

Psalms 91:2 LB

Trust in the Lord with all your heart. Your heart is the innermost part of you, the citadel of your personality, the core and motivation of your being. It is the deepest part of your spiritual life, the part that makes everything else tick—and that part of you must be centered totally on God.

David put it another way when he said, "My heart is fixed, O God . . ." (Psalms 57:7). If a ship is being guided by a directional instrument, that instrument must be fixed on a course, or the ship will be plowing through the sea in an aimless fashion. The guidance system of that ship must be fixed.

It will do you no good to have your heart fixed on personal wealth or other selfish motives, while at the same time you claim to have fixed it on God. Your heart must be zeroed in on one target—God Almighty —and the relationship must be one of absolute trust.

PAT ROBERTSON

Our prayer for today:

Almighty God, create in our hearts a complete trust in You, we pray. Keep us from clinging to personal desires. May we keep our eyes on You, our Father, who guides us each day.

July 4

And ye shall know the truth, and the truth shall make you free.

John 8:32

In Concord, Massachussetts, in 1761, a rousing speech was made by James Otis, a former advocate of the King of England. John Adams declared that Otis's words "breathed into this Nation the breath of life!" It was the beginning of the American Revolution. The cost was high, but liberty was won. All through history, sacrifices have been made so that men and women might live in freedom.

On a Cross, almost two thousand years ago, Jesus Christ gave His life so that we could be free from the condemnation of sin. His sacrifice meant that we could know eternal life and live in the freedom of His love and forgiveness. Freedom of mind, body, and soul is easy to take for granted each day, until we remember those living in countries where every freedom has been crushed by the heel of an enslaving ideology.

—J.W.B.

Our prayer for today:

Lord Jesus, we thank You that we can live in freedom. We think of those who at this very moment are living under oppression. May they know the liberation of Your love in their hearts and souls.

July 5

A word fitly spoken is like apples of gold in pictures of silver.

Proverbs 25:11

Jack and I were sitting in a coffee shop one afternoon, discussing the question of priorities. He asked me how I knew I was number one after God on his priority list. I recalled several incidents that more than proved to me my status in his life, such as the time he canceled a business trip to take care of me when I had caught the mumps from our daughter Lynn and was very ill. I looked like a horror at the time, but he didn't even comment on my grotesque appearance, which added saintliness to his virtues.

When I asked his question back to him, he said, "I know that I am on the top of your priority list *because you tell me.* I may not be greatly responsive when you compliment me [sometimes he acts embarrassed, or responds in a more subdued way than I would], but I really appreciate all the nice things you say."

Solomon stated that "a man hath joy by the answer of his mouth and a word spoken in due season, how good is it" (Proverbs 15:23 KJV).

Joy comes into our lives and marriages as we learn to speak many "good words" to those we love, but especially to that one God has chosen to be our partner for life.

JACK and CAROLE MAYHALL

Our prayer for today:

Father, forgive us for the times we do not tell each other how much we care and appreciate the joys we share.

July 6

Now Adam knew Eve his wife. . . .

Genesis 4:1 RSV

The deepest human need is to be *known* and *loved.* For most people the potential fulfillment of that need is found in the close and covenanted relationship of husband and wife. Communication—knowing and being known in depth—is one of the greatest joys of sex and of marriage itself. When a marriage has *soul,* and two people are growing together in their total relationship, there are moments of union that transcend both word and touch. Call it "mystical" if you wish . . . I call it "communicating." It is not an everyday occurrence, nor does it need to be. But once it happens, it leaves its mark not only on the marriage but on all of the couple's life.

COLLEEN and LOUIS EVANS, JR.

Our prayer for today:

Thank You, our Father, for this relationship we share. Let there be honesty, understanding, and a deep love that brings with it the joy of complete communication.

July 7

> . . . live together in harmony, live together in love, as though you had only one mind and one spirit between you.
>
> Philippians 2:2 PHILLIPS

There is absolutely nothing sinful about enjoying sex. You are married now—enjoy yourself. Let yourself go. You are free to enjoy yourself.

Know that the way to enjoy yourself is never to seek self-satisfaction, but always to seek the satisfaction of someone else. Happiness always comes as a by-product. If you ever set out with the intention of finding pleasure for yourself, you will run into all kinds of frustrations. Live to bring fulfillment, joy and pleasure to your mate, and you will experience the wonderful happy feeling that comes when you see that you have brought true joy to some wonderful person whom you love.

ROBERT H. SCHULLER

Our prayer for today:

Lord, as we see joy in the face of our loved one, we experience true happiness. Thank You for the enjoyment we find in each other.

July 8

Pray ye therefore. . . .

                                                        Matthew 9:38

When we pray for others the Spirit of God works in the unconscious domain of their being that we know nothing about, and the one we are praying for knows nothing about, but after the passing of time the conscious life of the one prayed for begins to show signs of unrest and disquiet. We may have spoken until we are worn out, but have never come anywhere near, and we have given up in despair. But if we have been praying, we find on meeting them one day that there is the beginning of a softening in an enquiry and a desire to know something. It is that kind of intercession that does most damage to Satan's kingdom. It is so slight, so feeble in its initial stages that if reason is not wedded to the light of the Holy Spirit, we will never obey it. It seems stupid to think that we can pray and all that will happen, but remember to Whom we pray; we pray to a God Who understands the unconscious depths of personality about which we know nothing, and He has told us to pray.

                                                OSWALD CHAMBERS

Our prayer for today:

Lord God, let us keep praying and *believing*—for those our hearts have been burdened to pray for. We can lose hope of seeing an answer so easily. Forgive our wavering faith. We praise You, that in *Your* perfect time, You will answer!

July 9

For he knoweth our frame. . . .

Psalms 103:14

In my living room is a beautiful glass ornament given to me by my husband, Bill, on our fifteenth wedding anniversary. The inscription by Alfred, Lord Tennyson reads: "More things are wrought by prayer than this world dreams of."

Each time I look at this, I am reminded of the many times in our marriage that God has answered our prayers, and my heart is filled with thankfulness. If I am going through a difficult time, this phrase speaks to me again of God's faithfulness.

Often I have thought a situation to be almost hopeless, but as I have cried out to the Lord in prayer, He has answered, in His time. What seemed hopeless has been turned into a beautiful victory for Him. There have been other times when He has not answered my requests, but has shown me a much better way.

The communion that comes when we are totally honest as we pray is a glorious experience. He knows us: our thoughts, our motives; yet so often we try to hide all that is on our hearts from Him. In doing so, we miss so much. Our Lord is always waiting to commune with us. We are never alone in sorrow, conflict, or joy.

—J.W.B.

Our prayer for today:

Lord, we cannot hide from You. Forgive us when our prayers do not come from deep within our hearts. Teach us to pray in such a way that we will always know the joy of Your close fellowship.

July 10

For this cause we . . . do not cease to pray for you. . . .

Colossians 1:9

Pray without Ceasing.—Does that refer to prayer for ourselves or others? To both. It is because many confine it to themselves that they fail so in practising it. It is only when the branch gives itself to bear fruit, more fruit, much fruit, that it can live a healthy life, and expect a rich inflow of sap. The death of Christ brought Him to the place of everlasting intercession. Your death with Him to sin and self sets you free from the care of self, and elevates you to the dignity of intercessor—one who can get life and blessing from God for others. Know your calling; begin this your work. Give yourself wholly to it, and ere you know you will be finding something of this *"Praying Always"* within you.

ANDREW MURRAY

Our prayer for today:

Use us to intercede for others, Lord. May our prayer life deepen and become more and more a natural conversation with the One whom we adore.

July 11

And hope maketh not ashamed. . . .

Romans 5:5

Love hopes all things. How extravagant is Paul's song! How absurd, in the face of tough realities and expert prognoses, even to speak of such unlimited hope! But love, the power that suffers long without setting limits, is also the power that keeps hoping without setting due dates. Despair comes from deadlines set too early and hope defined too narrowly. Hope fails when love is a demand instead of a gift. Agapic love lets things and people be, and in the gift of letting things and people be, love becomes a power that creates a hope that will not disappoint us.

LEWIS B. SMEDES

Our prayer for today:

Your hope invades our hearts and keeps us from despair, Lord. Help us not to limit each other with demanding love, we pray.

July 12

> Can a woman forget her sucking child, that she should not have
> compassion on the son of her womb? yea, they may forget, yet will
> I not forget thee. Behold I have graven thee upon the palms of my
> hands. . . .
>
> Isaiah 49:15, 16

My mother tells of spending a long day at the doctor's office, taking
those dreary tests that are generally worse than the illness for which
they are testing. At the end of the day, as everyone was finishing the
day's records, one of the dressing room doors burst open, and a rather
large man, draped in a rather small smock, bellowed at the amazed
office workers, "When is someone going to get to me?"

Do you ever feel like that? I do! When is God going to get to me?
Has He forgotten me? Noah may have wondered that as he waited for
over a year in an ark full of undiapered animals! Have you figured that
since God didn't honor your plan and your timing, He had no more
use for your person?

Sometimes ignoring our plan is the best thing God can do for us, and
sometimes delaying our plan is the most protective thing He can do for
us. Wait for God's plan. . . . He won't forget you.

                                                    JEANNETTE CLIFT

Our prayer for today:

How often, Lord, we fret and fume because we feel neglected. Forgive
us. Help us to be ready when You call us, Lord God.

July 13

> And why worry about a speck in the eye of a brother when you
> have a board in your own?
>
> Matthew 7:3 LB

Some individuals seem to think that a bonus privilege of marriage is
to be constantly criticizing the other. At a dinner recently, one wife

spent the whole meal correcting her husband. He made too much noise when he ate, he didn't tear his bread in half before eating it, and he spilled some coffee over into his saucer. She acted as though she had been given the divine appointment to be her husband's critic. Interestingly, she didn't criticize any of the others at the table.

A critical attitude is a result of sin and selfishness. The average Christian critic avoids self-examination; it is much too painful.

In a marriage, the one who is always criticized has a tendency to "clam up," and before long, communication is blocked. The joy of growing together from experience to experience is lost.

—B.B.

Our prayer for today:

We miss so much in our marriage, Lord, when we become judgmental of each other. Help us to deal with each other's faults in a spirit of love and consideration.

July 14

> Thou believest that there is one God; thou doest well: the devils also believe, and tremble. But wilt thou know, O vain man, that faith without works is dead?
>
> James 2:19, 20

There is a drugstore in America, which, it is claimed, has been open night and day for twenty-six years, and during that period a million prescriptions have been made up. The front windows of the shop are packed with the prescriptions, written on all kinds of paper, and over the front entrance stands the slogan, "Trusted a million times!" That is an effective advertisement; but it also carries with it a lesson in faith.

Think, for a moment, what happens when we are ill. We call in a doctor, and he writes out a prescription. We look at the hieroglyphics, and have no idea what they mean, yet we send down to the druggist and have the medicine made up, although it may be deadly poison for all we know to the contrary; and when it arrives we exercise perfect faith in swallowing it, according to the instructions.

Now, in the spiritual realm, this is just the kind of faith God is looking for: a faith that not only believes that His Son Jesus Christ is the Saviour of the world (that may be mere intellectual assent), but a faith that takes Him personally for salvation, and believes on His Name.

A. LINDSAY GLEGG

Our prayer for today:

Father, we believe that Your Son, Jesus Christ, is our Savior and Lord. In faith we received Him, and in faith we live each day in the power of His name!

July 15

> As one whom his mother comforteth, so will I comfort you. . . .
>
> Isaiah 66:13

Every morning the sun rises to warm the earth. If it were to fail to shine for just one minute, all life on the earth would die. The rains come to water the earth. There is fertility in the soil, life in the seeds, oxygen in the air. The providence of God is about us in unbelievable abundance every moment. But so often we just take it for granted.

With infinite love and compassion our Lord understood the human predicament. He had deep empathy with people; He saw their needs, their weaknesses, their desires, and their hurts. He understood and was concerned for people. Every word He spoke was uttered because He saw a need for that word in some human life. His concern was always to uplift and never to tear down, to heal and never hurt, to save and not condemn.

CHARLES L. ALLEN

Our prayer for today:

Our Lord, thank You for Your comfort and love. As we see evidence all around us of Your caring, we praise You! Give us Your concern and care—not only for each other, but also for those around us, we pray.

July 16

   . . . And the teaching of kindness is on her tongue.

Proverbs 31:26 NAS

In joining two people together as husband and wife, God has arranged that there should be subjection and love in the family. He has not asked the husband and wife to find and correct each other's faults. He has not set up husbands to be instructors to their wives, or wives to be teachers to their husbands. A husband need not change his wife or a wife her husband. Whatever the manner of person you marry, you must expect to live with that for life. Married people should learn to know when to close their eyes. They should learn to love and not try to correct.

WATCHMAN NEE

Our prayer for today:

   Our Father, let us show kindness to each other. As we face the complexities of our daily life, we ask Your love to guide us.

July 17

   . . . Thou shalt love the Lord thy God with all thy heart, and with all thy soul, and with all thy mind.

Matthew 22:37

This is the commandment of the great God, and he cannot command the impossible. Love is a fruit in season at all times, and within reach of every hand. Anyone may gather it and no limit is set. Everyone can reach this love through meditation, spirit of prayer and sacrifice, by an intense inner life.

MOTHER TERESA

Our prayer for today:

Without Your love in our hearts, Lord Jesus, we know it is impossible to keep God's commandments. Fill us with Your love, so that we may love as we should.

July 18

Let marriage be held in honor among all, and let the marriage bed be undefiled. . . .

Hebrews 13:4 RSV

The marriage bed is something very special. It provides a unique means of refreshment and delight. A place of comfort, strengthening, invigoration, communion, and nurture. A place to which a husband and wife return again and again to experience the wonder of merging themselves with one another, the joy of being fused together, the thrill of physically expressing the deepest emotions of their hearts. God intended sex to be that way. And so the marriage bed must be kept undefiled. It must be guarded from anything that would detract from or spoil a couple's love and unity. Obviously, this means that there must be no room for unfaithfulness. Sex is to be reserved for a husband and wife alone. Their bodies belong only to each other and to God.

LETHA SCANZONI

Our prayer for today:

Almighty God, let us never abuse the gift You have given us. Keep our hearts, minds, and bodies completely faithful to You and to each other.

July 19

. . . How God anointed Jesus of Nazareth with the Holy Ghost and with power: who went about doing good. . . .

Acts 10:38

Love is patience . . . love understands, and therefore waits. Love is kindness. Have you ever noticed how much of Christ's life was spent in doing kind things for others? He spent a great proportion of His time simply in making people happy, in doing good turns to people . . . God has put in our power the happiness of those about us, and that is largely to be accomplished by the way we treat them —kindly or otherwise.

HENRY DRUMMOND

Our prayer for today:

Lord Jesus, wherever You went, You showed kindness and concern. How we need those same qualities in our lives. Let them begin with the way we treat each other.

July 20

> But the Comforter, which is the Holy Ghost, whom the Father will send in my name, he shall teach you all things, and bring all things to your remembrance, whatsoever I have said unto you.

John 14:26

Remember *The Miracle Worker,* that moving, true story of Helen Keller—blind, deaf, and dumb after an early childhood disease and isolated in her dark and silent world? One day Miss Anne Sullivan moved into her life. The child Helen Keller could not know then that the love and patience and wisdom of her new teacher could change her from an "animal" into one of history's great human beings, but that is the difference which Anne Sullivan made when she came into Helen Keller's life.

This is what the Holy Spirit does for you and me. He moves into our lives, unpacks, and stays forever. He has come to release us from our slavery to animal passions and transforms us into sons and daughters of God. It will take our lifetimes. It will mean conflict and tension and hard decisions. But He is there to comfort us along the way. He encourages and loves us when we grow weary or afraid. He disciplines us when we get lazy or forgetful. He forgives us when we fail. He helps us change our values and rearrange our priorities. He is our Counselor, our Friend, our Teacher, our Guide. He brings us joy.

MEL WHITE

Our prayer for today:

Almighty God, Your Holy Spirit comforts our hearts. In all the conflicts of daily life, You are there to bring us joy and strength.

July 21

. . . love one another, as I have loved you.

John 15:12

God's formula for a marriage that works is so beautifully described in Ephesians 5:28–33 (LB):

That is how husbands should treat their wives, loving them as part of themselves. For since a man and his wife are now one, a man is really doing himself a favor and loving himself when he loves his wife! No one hates his own body but lovingly cares for it, just as Christ cares for his body the church, of which we are parts. (That the husband and wife are one body is proved by the Scripture which says, "A man must leave his father and mother when he marries, so that he can be perfectly joined to his wife, and the two shall be one.") I know this is hard to understand, but it is an illustration of the way we are parts of the body of Christ. So again I say, a man must love his wife as a part of himself; and the wife must see to it that she deeply respects her husband—obeying, praising, and honoring him.

No marriage counselor on earth can write better copy than that!

—B.B.

Our prayer for today:

Dear Lord, because we are one in You, help us this day to realize the harmony we can enjoy. Let us learn to love each other as You loved

us: unquestioningly, unselfishly, willing to sacrifice everything. Thank
You, Lord Jesus.

July 22

> And the Lord make you to increase and abound in love one toward
> another. . . .
>
> 1 Thessalonians 3:12

When a husband and wife cease to perform their services to each
other in love and begin to carry them out from a sense of duty alone,
the marriage tie becomes enslaving, and acts that were once a joy
become "crosses."

Many Christians think that taking up the cross means doing something they ought to do but dislike doing—and they may even feel that
such distasteful service is particularly pleasing to God. But would any
man be pleased if his wife said to him every morning as he left for work,
"I am going to clean the house and cook dinner for you today, but I
want you to know that I despise doing these chores"? No wonder Paul
was alarmed when he found that this legalistic spirit was creeping into
the churches in Galatia.

Legalistic Christians do not actually deny Jesus; they only seek to
add something to Him. Their idea is "Jesus *and*. . . . " Perhaps it is Jesus
and good works, Jesus and deep emotion, Jesus and correct doctrine,
or Jesus and certain religious rites. These things may be good in themselves, and *are* good when they are the fruits of salvation, but to add
*any*thing to Christ as a *requirement* for salvation is to deny His com-
pleteness and exalt oneself.

HANNAH WHITALL SMITH
Paraphrased by
CATHERINE JACKSON

Our prayer for today:

Dear Lord, we remember when we took our wedding vows. It seemed
nothing would ever become just a duty, but everything would remain

an act of love toward each other. Forgive the inward feelings that take away that first joy we knew. Teach us Your unselfish love.

July 23

> Confess your faults one to another, and pray for one another, that ye may be healed. . . .
>
> James 5:16

When one person begins to be dishonest with the other, then meaningful communication breaks down. What would be a biblical term for being honest with the Lord? "If we confess our sins, he is faithful and just to forgive us our sins, and to cleanse us from all unrighteousness" (1 John 1:9). That's nothing more than being honest with God. It's ridiculous not to be honest with God; He knows what's going on anyway. Yet, God wants a basic honesty from us if we are going to have meaningful communication.

CURTIS C. MITCHELL

Our prayer for today:

Our Father, in all our relationships and with You, may we be completely honest. Let there be no hiding the truth or drawing back from confessing our faults and needs.

July 24

> And the glory which thou gavest me I have given them; that they may be one, even as we are one.
>
> John 17:22

Let God speak to you and listen to Him. When you are together, then open up your Bibles and read a portion together. Talk about it—what He says to you. Allow yourselves to be comforted, counselled and guided by God.

Then fold your hands together and spread out your worries before God. He knows the way. He will take you by the hand and lead you. He has brought you together. He will hinder the attempt of people to separate you. Believe that with all your hearts.

Don't be embarrassed to pray in front of one another. You will have to overcome this feeling of embarrassment. Now is your chance to learn it. Now you will see if you can talk about everything—also about your faith. A common faith is the most solid foundation for a marriage. If you build your house on this rock, then no storm can destroy it.

WALTER TROBISCH

Our prayer for today:

Lord, help us to pray openly together. May Your Word become so entrenched in us that we will constantly look to You for guidance and wisdom. Thank You, Lord Jesus, for the gift of our love.

July 25

> The Lord shall preserve thee from all evil: he shall preserve thy soul.
>
> Psalms 121:7

God's plan for us is so practical—and so wonderful!

Marriage offers real safety in a world filled with questionable relationships. Marriage commitments create a hedge against the many attacks that Satan would mount against our moral foundations. Thank God for the security and stability that we can know as we allow Him to cradle and protect us by His statutes and holy institutions.

The church and the family aren't "prison compounds"; they're God's walled cities, places of refuge and protection!

PAT BOONE

Our prayer for today:

Thank You, Lord, for our marriage, which protects us from the attacks of Satan. As we yield ourselves and our house to You, we find a peaceful refuge.

July 26

> Finally, be ye all of one mind, having compassion one of another,
> love as brethren, be pitiful, be courteous.

1 Peter 3:8

A little thought will show you how vastly your own happiness depends on the way other people bear themselves toward you. The looks and tones at your breakfast table, the conduct of your fellow-workers or employers, the faithful or unreliable men you deal with, what people say to you on the street . . . the letters you get, the friends or foes you meet,—these things make up very much of the pleasure or misery of your day. Turn the idea around, and remember that just so much are you adding to the pleasure or the misery of other people's days. And this is the half of the matter which you can control. Whether any particular day shall bring to you more of happiness or of suffering is largely beyond your power to determine. Whether each day of your life shall *give* happiness or suffering rests with yourself.

GEORGE S. MERRIAM

Our prayer for today:

This day, and all those that follow, may we bring happiness to those we come in contact with, Lord Jesus. Help us to deal with others as You, in Your infinite mercy, have dealt with us.

July 27

> For our light affliction, which is but for a moment, worketh for us
> a far more exceeding and eternal weight of glory.

2 Corinthians 4:17

God allows our suffering:

That we might be prepared to comfort others.
That we might not trust in ourselves.
That we might learn to give thanks in everything.

Don't doubt for a moment that circumstances of suffering are used of God to shape you and conform you into the "image of His Son . . .". *Nothing* enters your life accidentally—remember that. There is no such thing as "luck" or "coincidence" or "blind faith" to the child of God. Behind our every experience is our loving, sovereign Lord. He is continually working things out according to His infinite plan and purpose. And that includes our suffering.

CHARLES R. SWINDOLL

Our prayer for today:

Our loving Lord, through our suffering, we know You are allowing us to become people who can reach out to others. As we receive Your comfort, prepare our hearts, we pray, so that we may serve those You love.

July 28

> . . . walk as children of light. . . . Proving what is acceptable unto the Lord.
>
> Ephesians 5:8, 10

For the Christian, self-acceptance begins with the knowledge of his full acceptance by God who knows each life as it really is, an acceptance based on the reconciling work of Christ. Through the wonder of divine grace and forgiveness, one is able to "accept His acceptance." It is but a short step, then, to accept the husband or wife as a person who also is accepted by God. These are the links in the chain of acceptance. So if you have trouble accepting your mate, examine your own measure of self-acceptance. And if your mate finds it difficult to accept you, then perhaps he or she needs reinforcement for a flagging self-image. Step back and look at your conflict. See if it may possibly provide a clue to a deeper problem of self-acceptance—yours or your mate's. It may relieve the urgency and tension of other problems just to realize that there is a more significant area to work on, and that you can work on this together.

DWIGHT HERVEY SMALL

Our prayer for today:

Lord Jesus, thank You for accepting us as we are. Our lives are far from what they should be; yet You love us. Teach us to love each other and ourselves, we pray.

July 29

Dearly beloved, avenge not yourselves. . . .

Romans 12:19

There are seasons when to be *still* demands immeasurably higher strength than to act. Composure is often the highest result of power. To the vilest and most deadly charges Jesus responded with deep, unbroken silence, such as excited the wonder of the judge and the spectators. To the grossest insults, the most violent ill-treatment and mockery that might well bring indignation into the feeblest heart, He responded with voiceless complacent calmness. Those who are unjustly accused, and causelessly ill-treated, know that tremendous strength is necessary to keep silence to God.

MARGARET BOTTOME

Our prayer for today:

Lord Jesus, our first instinct is to fight back when we are unjustly accused. Let us look to You—our supreme example—for even on the Cross, You asked forgiveness for those who had so cruelly treated You.

July 30

> . . . "Look! There is the Lamb of God who takes away the world's
> sin!"

> John 1:29 LB

At Calvary He who was God, very God died for us *physically* to
atone for sins done in the flesh: He died morally, being made sin
for us who knew no sin, in order that we might be made right with
His righteousness *morally;* He died *spiritually* in total separation
from His Father, which was to taste the awfulness of hell itself, to
atone for our spiritual wrongdoing and heal our separation from a
loving God.

It is on the basis of this titanic transaction, beyond the capacity of
any man to fully plumb, that we are invited to receive Him as divine
royalty. We are urged to accept Him as the only way of reconciling
ourselves to a loving God. We receive Him as our Savior.

W. PHILLIP KELLER

Our prayer for today:

Lord Jesus Christ, when we remember the agony endured by You for
our sins, we are grieved and humbled. Forgive us for the many times
we fail You. Thank You, Lord, for Your great love.

July 31

> . . . I pray God your whole spirit and soul and body be preserved
> blameless unto the coming of our Lord Jesus Christ.

> 1 Thessalonians 5:23

Even though we are rapidly approaching the time when the Anti-
christ will try to take over the world, I am not afraid. For I have an
even greater promise of the constant Presence of Jesus who is greater
than anything Satan can throw against me.

The Apostle Peter said, "Because, my dear friends, you have a hope like this before you, I urge you to make certain that such a day will find you at peace with God and man, clean and blameless in his sight" (2 Peter 3:14 PHILLIPS).

Surrender to the Lord Jesus Christ must not be partial—but total. Only when we repent and turn away from our sins (using His power, of course) does He fill us with His Holy Spirit. The fruit of the Holy Spirit makes us right with God and God's love in us makes us right with men. Through that we can forgive—even love —our enemies.

Jesus Himself makes us ready for His Coming.

CORRIE TEN BOOM

Our prayer for today:

May our lives be prepared for the day when You return, Lord Jesus! The hope and joy Your coming brings fills us with the courage to face the future. Thank You, Lord.

AUGUST

August 1

. . . "love each other as much as I love you."

John 15:12 LB

It's been said that if a couple doesn't grow together they grow apart. But for the couple who have in all seriousness said their vows before God and in the presence of witnesses, the possibility of growing apart need not be allowed. It need never be something which "happens to" them, as though they were bystanders injured by some force which they were powerless to protect themselves from. They have willed to love and live together. They stand, not helpless, but in relation to God, each responsible to fulfill his vows to the other. Each determines to do the will of God so that together they move toward "the measure of the stature of the fullness of Christ."

ELISABETH ELLIOT

Our prayer for today:

Father, may each day draw us closer together, as we rely completely on Your love.

August 2

. . . how I need your help, especially in my own home. . . .

Psalms 101:2 LB

Many homes are on the rocks today because God has been left out of the domestic picture. With the continual clash of personalities in a domestic pattern, there must be an integrating force, and the Living God is that Force! Many couples think that if they have a better home, get a better job, or live in a different neighborhood their domestic life will be happier. No! The secret of domestic happiness is to let God, the party of the third part in the marriage contract, have His rightful place in the home. Make peace with Him, and then you can be a real peacemaker in the home.

BILLY GRAHAM

Our prayer for today:

Lord Jesus Christ, the Prince of Peace, may Your loving presence be always in our home. Do not let us shut You out, as the days become filled with the pressures of everyday living.

August 3

And the Lord make you to increase and abound in love one toward another. . . .

1 Thessalonians 3:12

I met you years ago
when
of all the men
I knew,
you,
I hero-worshiped
then:
you are my husband now . . .
my husband!
and from my home
(your arms),
I turn to look
down the long trail of years
to where I met you first

and hero-worshiped,
and I would smile;
. . . I know you better now:
the faults,
the odd preferments,
the differences
that make you *you.*
That other me
—so young,
so far away—
saw you
and hero-worshiped
but never *knew;*
while I,
grown wiser
with the closeness of these years,
hero-worship, too!

RUTH BELL GRAHAM

Our prayer for today:

Father, we remember the day we met and looked into each other's eyes. Our love grows each day, and as the years fly by, help us to keep that young, tender love alive in our hearts.

August 4

A word fitly spoken is like apples of gold in pictures of silver.

Proverbs 25:11

Why do some husbands or wives find it easy to compliment those outside their home, yet they find it so difficult to praise each other? Some men tell their secretaries how nice they look more often than they tell their wives. Some women compliment the "handyman" who is married to the lady next door more often than they build up their husbands.

No husband or wife ever gets praised too often by his or her partner.

A thoughtful remark early in the morning can set the tone for the rest of the day.

Some partners think finding fault, instead of building up, keeps the other "humble." All of us have things about us that can be criticized. Our weaknesses are indelible on our minds, so we don't need to be reminded of them.

Make it a daily habit in your marriage to say several things of praise to the one you love. A wife who is told she is attractive, for instance, makes special effort to keep herself that way. A man who is told he is special wants to live up to his wife's evaluation.

—B.B.

Our prayer for today:

Father, help is to remember that encouragement and praise are two strong elements in making our lives together even happier. May we realize the value of building each other up.

August 5

. . . Let patience have her perfect work. . . .

James 1:4

The exercise of patience involves a continual practice of the presence of God; for we may be come upon at any moment for an almost heroic display of good temper, and it is a short road to unselfishness, for nothing is left to self; all that seems to belong most intimately to self; to be self's private property, such as time, home, and rest, are invaded by these continual trials of patience. The family is full of such opportunities.

F. W. FABER

Our prayer for today:

Lord, we have so little patience of our own! It seems there are so often unwelcome interruptions and problems that invade our home. Help us to overcome our impatience by constantly being aware of Your presence in our lives.

August 6

> If you are angry, don't sin by nursing your grudge. Don't let the
> sun go down with you still angry—get over it quickly.

> Ephesians 4:26 LB

It happens to all couples . . . it has happened to us . . . these
differences, these misunderstandings . . . and many times we have
walked the beaches—or the parks or the city streets—late at night and
even into the next sunrise, because we knew that we had to make things
right between us. That coming back together has to take priority over
everything, no matter what else has to wait its turn. Neither of us is able
to function well with that terrible wrenching feeling deep inside that
comes when we misunderstand each other . . . it's like being pulled apart
physically, which of course it is in every other sense. And so, we do
without some sleep, and the next day we're pretty tired, but our peace
has been won. . . . We understand each other again, and so it's okay.
There is that wonderful feeling of healing and wholeness inside and we
don't mind being sleepy.

. . . we can be shaped by a love that has far greater power. And
we don't have to wonder whether we're angry or irritable . . . because
God's love is *never* touchy!

COLLEEN TOWNSEND EVANS

Our prayer for today:

Dear Lord, thank You, that we can come to You with our differences, our hurts. Take away our self-righteousness and fill our hearts
with Your love and forgiveness.

August 7

> I, even I, am he that comforteth you. . . .

> Isaiah 51:12

It is Paul, the apostle of consolation, who gave us the delightful
exhortation, *"Comfort one another"* (*see* 1 Thessalonians 4:18; 2 Corinthians 2:1–4). But we can only experience this mutual comfort as,

personally, each believer is comforted by God through the Scriptures. The lack of that warm, heartening, and consoling fellowship among many believers today is because of the lack of the everlasting consolation of Jesus within each heart. When every believer walks in the comfort of the Holy Spirit what else can they do but comfort one another when they meet?

The heart that has not suffered has little comfort to give to those who weep and suffer in a sorrowing world, because sympathy is born of experience. We are only capable of comforting one another, when, individually, we know the joy of divine comfort.

HERBERT LOCKYER

Our prayer for today:

Your comfort embraces our lives, Lord Jesus. Because we have been sustained by You, we can console each other. Keep us tender and ever aware of the needs around us.

August 8

> Make haste, my beloved, and be thou like to a roe or to a young
> hart upon the mountains of spices.

Song of Solomon 8:14

The Song of Solomon is a book extolling the erotic delights of marriage. To allegorize this Scripture is to overlook the obvious message that sex is one of God's good gifts.

To the end that men and women are to enjoy maximum sex, the Bible restricts intercourse to marriage. Within the secure commitment of wedlock, each partner is to freely give and receive sex. Since each spouse has the right to sexual satisfaction, they each give selflessly of themselves to bring pleasure to the other. They neither suppress nor repress sex in the context of their marriage.

PAMELA HEIM

Our prayer for today:

Lord, may each part of our marriage glorify You. We ask that in our physical lives, selfless love will be the dominant factor.

August 9

> Order my steps in thy word: and let not any iniquity have dominion over me.

> Psalms 119:133

When Christian couples bow to the authority of God's Word, they commit themselves to certain goals and to the means of reaching them. In their personal character they choose to grow in likeness to Jesus Christ, which in their marriage they choose to let Christ be the Head. For committed Christians to seek their own way is not only allowing for conflict and competitiveness, but is a contradiction of Christian commitment. For to the degree that God's Word is authoritative in the life of a couple, to that degree their individual wills are subordinate to the will of God.

DWIGHT HERVEY SMALL

Our prayer for today:

May we grow in Your likeness, Lord Jesus, as we read and obey Your Word. Let our love, our ambitions, our hopes and dreams be guided by the Scriptures.

August 10

> . . . What therefore God hath joined together, let not man put asunder.

> Matthew 19: 6

Just this morning, my heart sank as a Christian friend told me that, after forty years of marriage, his mother and father (also Christians) had divorced.

What went wrong? Because there were defects in their lives, and problems in the everyday effort of *staying* married, it did not make them any less married.

One of the great purposes of marriage is the growth that can be experienced. In practice, husband and wife discover that their lives have to be constantly surrendered to each other so that, through encouragement and help, both may grow in the likeness and image of Christ.

Romans 5:5 (RSV) says, ". . . God's love has been poured into our hearts through the Holy Spirit which has been given to us."

Two people, living a love (in Christ) that is unselfish, giving, and forgiving, are able to communicate a very special love to each other, regardless of the circumstances surrounding them. But they must *both* want it.

—B.B.

Our prayer for today:

Jesus, as we grow together as Your children, let us look beyond our defects to You, who only is perfection. Together may our lives be completely yielded to our Savior and Lord.

August 11

For God so loved the world. . . .

John 3:16

The great majority of Christians have never been able to believe that when Christ said the whole duty of man resolved itself into loving God and our neighbor, he meant just that. It seems too simple, too obvious. And, furthermore, there is the question of who is our neighbor. This was put to him slyly by a lawyer who hoped to trick him into differentiating between Jews and Gentiles. Instead, Christ told the parable of the Good Samaritan, using for its setting the road from Jerusalem to Jericho which, to this day, in its wildness, its remoteness and weird desolation, gives rise to thoughts of banditry such as befell the traveller who fell among thieves. This man's neighbor, Christ forces the lawyer to admit, was surely the Samaritan who helped him rather than the priest and the Levite who passed by on the other side. In Christ's estimation, our neighbor is everyone.

MALCOLM MUGGERIDGE

Our prayer for today:

Give us Your love for our neighbors, Lord Jesus. May we be completely stripped of prejudice and any superior attitudes. Forgive us, Lord.

August 12

> For if ye forgive men their trespasses, your heavenly Father will also forgive you: But if ye forgive not men their trespasses, neither will your Father forgive your trespasses.
>
> Matthew 6:14, 15

Jesus' teaching on forgiveness is something like an automobile. You dare not run your car on steel rims with no rubber tires, or electricity may come into it and kill you. But with rubber tires the car is insulated and electricity cannot flow out of you: so it will not flow into you. If it can't get out of the car, it can't get into the car. And if forgiveness can't get out of you, it is not going to get into you. Forgiveness is a requirement of God that is unalterable. It is the plain teaching of our Lord Jesus and has never been revoked. Where there is unforgiveness, there will be no grace flowing into the soul of a marriage.

JOHN R. BISAGNO

Our prayer for today:

Father, this day we search our hearts to see if there are any hidden resentments. We ask that Your Holy Spirit will show us if there is anyone we have not forgiven. Give us the grace to forgive, we pray.

August 13

> . . . let us stop just saying we love people; let us really love them, and show it by our actions.
>
> 1 John 3:18 LB

As memory scans the past, above and beyond all the transitory pleasures of life, there leap forward those supreme hours when you have been enabled to do unnoticed kindnesses to those round about you, things too trifling to speak about, but which you feel have entered into your eternal life. I have seen almost all the beautiful things God has made; I have enjoyed almost every pleasure that He has planned for man; and yet as I look back I see standing out above all the life that has gone, four or five short experiences when the love of God reflected itself in some imitation, some small act of love of mine, and these seem to be the things which alone of all one's life abide. Everything else in all our lives is transitory. Every other good is visionary. But the acts of love which no man knows about, or can ever know about—they never fail.

HENRY DRUMMOND

Our prayer for today:

Lord, may this day be filled with acts of love that do not seek reward or praise but are done only to see the joy on the faces of loved ones and others. Let all be done to glorify You!

August 14

> Blessed is the man unto whom the Lord imputeth not iniquity, and in whose spirit there is no guile.
>
> Psalms 32:2

Communication involves more than words. Each word that is spoken conveys a certain disposition through its tone or accompanying facial and physical gestures. As a matter of fact, words may not even be necessary for a mood or disposition to be recognized. What we call disposition the Bible calls spirit. The spirit of a man communicates more than most people realize, which is the reason for the warning to "take heed then, to your spirit, and let no one deal treacherously" with his mate (Malachi 2:15). It is crucial in the process of communication that you pay attention to your spirit and the spirit of your mate.

The goal of marriage is oneness. In a very real sense spiritual communication is the adhesive of marital oneness; it is essential that a couple strive to achieve spiritual unity, the blending of two spirits together with God.

TIM TIMMONS

Our prayer for today:

Our lives are entwined together in Your love, Lord. Teach us spiritual oneness, so we will experience that unity which comes from You, our Father and our God.

August 15

> . . . jealousy is cruel as the grave: the coals thereof are coals of fire, which hath a most vehement flame.

Song of Solomon 8:6

Peter was the object of sinful jealousy on several occasions. So was Paul, who because of the jealousy and envy of others, was arrested several times, imprisoned, stoned, exiled. He did not let this distract him from his ministry. . . .

But it's not only the famous who suffer through envy. Plenty of ordinary Christians have gone through agony because others have envied their courage and confidence. . . .

Jealousy has divided homes. It has come between husbands and wives, contradicting the Bible's claim that a wife is bone of her husband's bone, and flesh of his flesh. Envy and jealousy have brought ruin to prosperous cities and overthrown great nations.

So, let's remind ourselves that envy and jealousy are nothing but tricks of the mind, attitudes, self-induced fantasies; and let us put them from us.

CLEMENT OF ROME (A.D. 30–100)
Paraphrased by DAVID WINTER

Our prayer for today:

Father, You have given each of us gifts. May we not be jealous of each other, nor may we be the cause of hurting each other. Help us to realize we are one in You. Everything we achieve should enhance our marriage, Lord.

August 16

> . . . out of the abundance of the heart the mouth speaketh.

> Matthew 12:34

Tell God all that is in your heart, as one unloads one's heart to a dear friend. People who have no secrets from each other never want subjects of conversation; they do not weigh their words, because there is nothing to be kept back. Neither do they seek for something to say; they talk out of the abundance of their hearts, just what they think. Blessed are they who attain to such familiar, unreserved intercourse with God.

FRANÇOIS DE FENELON
(1651–1715)

Our prayer for today:

We speak to You today, Lord, knowing You are our Friend and our God. You are interested in every detail of our lives. In this quiet moment, we would take time to tell You all that is on our hearts. There is nothing secret from You, Father.

August 17

> . . . he will teach the ways that are right and best to those who humbly turn to him.

> Psalms 25:9 LB

Winston Churchill had little admiration for his political rival, Clement Atlee, and rarely had anything good to say about him. One day his friends were surprised, therefore, when he reputedly volunteered the information, "Clement Atlee is a very humble man." After a suitable pause he added with a Churchillian twinkle, "Of course, he has a lot to be humble about!"

It is not hard for human beings to adopt a humble attitude when we are conversant with the biblical teaching on the human condition and the divine remedy, because we have much to be humble about! There is no doubt that God expects this attitude. In fact, He reserves some of His strongest words for those who refuse to humble themselves. Paul not only found it possible to turn from his arrogant pharisaical attitudes but also took great delight in the way he had been humbled before God. He was even excited about being humble!

D. STUART BRISCOE

Our prayer for today:

Our Father, teach us humility, we pray. As we read in Your Word of Your Son, Jesus Christ, may we see the beauty of His humble life in contrast to the pride in ours. Forgive us, Father.

August 18

... to know the love of Christ, which passeth knowledge, that ye might be filled with all the fulness of God.

Ephesians 3:19

Jesus says to the believer, "Will you accept Me as your Beloved? Are you willing to follow Me into suffering and loneliness, and endure hardness for My sake, and to ask no reward but My smile of approval and My word of praise? Will you give Me absolute control of your life? Will you be content with pleasing Me and Me only? May I have My way with you in all things? Will you come into so close a union with Me as to make a separation from the world necessary? Will you accept Me as your Bridegroom and leave all others to cleave only to Me?"

He makes this offer of union with Himself to every believer. But not all say yes to Him. Some feel that their other loves and other interests are too precious to be cast aside. Although they don't miss heaven because of this decision, they miss an unspeakable present joy.

HANNAH WHITALL SMITH
Paraphrased by
CATHERINE JACKSON

Our prayer for today:

We accept You, Lord Jesus, as our beloved Bridegroom—head of our home and ruler of our hearts. We praise and love You, our Savior and Lord.

August 19

And this is life eternal, that they might know thee, the only true God, and Jesus Christ whom thou hast sent.

John 17:3

One thing . . . marriage has done for me. I can never again believe that religion is manufactured out of our unconscious starved desires and is a substitute for sex. For those few years H. [his wife Helen Joy] and I feasted on love; every mode of it—solemn and merry, romantic and realistic, sometimes as dramatic as a thunderstorm, sometimes as comfortable and unemphatic as putting on your soft slippers. No cranny of heart or body remained unsatisfied. If God were a substitute for love, we ought to have lost all interest in Him. Who'd bother about substitutes when he has the thing itself? But that isn't what happens. We both knew we wanted something besides one another—quite a different kind of something, a quite different kind of want. You might as well say that when lovers have one another, they will never want to read, or eat—or breathe. . . .

The most precious gift that marriage gave me was this constant impact of something very close and intimate yet all the time unmistakably other-resistant—in a word, real.

C. S. LEWIS

Our prayer for today:

Our lives together bring joy and satisfaction, Father, because You are the center of our marriage. You fill the vacuum and bring total joy!

August 20

. . . Martha, Martha, thou art careful and troubled about many things: But one thing is needful: and Mary hath chosen that good part. . . .

Luke 10:41, 42

Our life is very complicated, but Christ would bear every burden of your life. Christ says, "Pass it over to me, I will take it." Can you stand before the Lord today and say, "Here is my life, Lord, everything good and bad, every problem, every ambition I give it to You"? Hold your hands out and in your imagination let them hold everything. Then hold that everything up before God. Pass it all over to Him. Let Him take it.

HENRIETTA MEARS

Our prayer for today:

Lord Jesus, so often we bear the burdens when You wait for us to give them to You. In faith, we release all our anxieties and place them at Your loving feet, knowing You will hear our prayers.

August 21

For the husband is the head of the wife, even as Christ is the head of the church. . . .

Ephesians 5:23

No organization, whether it be marriage or business, functions well without a head or someone to act as a final authority. It is also rare for a business partnership to work smoothly when all the leaders have equal authority. Consequently, in God's wisdom, He has arranged for the smooth functioning of a marriage by giving the husband final accountability for the decisions: "For the husband is the head of the wife, as Christ also is the head of the church . . ." (Ephesians 5:23).

In most marriages there is a good bit of compromise and concession, but no matter how your household is run, situations will undoubtedly arise when there will be a difference of opinion. As Ruth Graham, wife of Dr. Billy Graham, once said, "If two people agree on everything, one of them is unnecessary." Consequently, there must be a final authority to deal with the problem and make the ultimate decision.

VONETTE Z. BRIGHT

Our prayer for today:

Lord Jesus, let our love for each other emulate the love that You gave to the church. When there are differences, may we remember to take them to You, our Mediator and Lord.

August 22

Rest in the Lord; wait patiently for him to act. . . .

Psalms 37:7 LB

Pain knocked upon my door and said
That she had come to stay,
And though I would not welcome her
But bade her go away,
She entered in.
Like my own shade
She followed after me,
And from her stabbing, stinging sword

No moment was I free.
And then one day another knocked
Most gently at my door.
I cried, "No, Pain is living here,
There is not room for more."
And then I heard His tender voice,
"'Tis I, be not afraid."
And from the day He entered in,
The difference it made!

MARTHA SNELL NICHOLSON

Our prayer for today:

Lord Jesus, help us not to be afraid if we have to suffer pain, whether physical or mental. May we be aware of Your presence and realize that through our pain, we may glorify You, our Savior and Lord.

August 23

Thou art worthy, O Lord, to receive glory and honour and power. . . .

Revelation 4:11

There are occasions in which your praying must take an attitude of sheer wonder and praise of God for God's sake. The New England farmer, sitting down to a sparse meal in lean times with his family, knew this when he prayed, "We thank Thee, Lord, that we have Thee and all this besides." Mother Teresa of Calcutta, the tiny nun who works among the poorest of the poor in India, is another who understands the meaning of adoration. Refusing all accolades, this contemporary saint said simply, "We have nothing. The greatness of God is that He has used this nothing to do something." Such a comment springs from an attitude of adoration of God. Have your prayers taken on the glow which stems from appreciating the Lord for His own sake? When they do, you will begin to comprehend the meaning of that quaint term, *loving the Lord.*

WILLIAM P. BARKER

Our prayer for today:

We are so blessed by Your love, Lord; yet so often we forget to tell You how much we love You. Our praise to You, the King of kings, comes from grateful and adoring hearts. Without You, we are nothing.

August 24

The Spirit of the Lord God is upon me . . . he hath sent me to bind up the brokenhearted. . . .

Isaiah 61: 1

The delicate, pink Victorian cup, given to my wife by her grandmother, fell to the floor, smashing into a hundred pieces. Gathering up each piece with loving care, Joan looked at me hopefully. "Can't it be mended? It means so much to me." That shattered cup still lies in a drawer, twenty-two years since the day it broke.

Unfortunately, many marriages are like that: abandoned because the effort needed to restore them seemed too great.

Jesus Christ, the One who said, "I will make all things new," is ready and available to apply His loving touch and care to every area of a marriage that is in need of repair, if only we'll let Him.

—B.B.

Our prayer for today:

Almighty God, let us be constantly aware that, in all our conflicts, we need not meet them *alone.* Your Holy Spirit is with us, helping us and allowing our lives to blend together.

August 25

I know the thoughts that I think toward you, saith the Lord, thoughts of peace, and not of evil, to give you an expected end.

Jeremiah 29:11

You are never to complain of your birth, your training, your employments, your hardships; never to fancy that you could be something if only you had a different lot and sphere assigned you. God understands His own plan, and He knows what you want a great deal better than you do. The very things that you most deprecate, as fatal limitations or obstructions, are probably what you most want. What you call hindrances, obstacles, discouragements, are probably God's opportunities.

H. BUSHNELL

Our prayer for today:

Dear God, thank You for the plans You have for us. Forgive the times we think of what *might* be, if we had this or that. You know what our needs are, and we thank You for Your loving kindness, Father.

August 26

> . . . yea, in the shadow of thy wings will I make my refuge, until these calamities be overpast.

Psalms 57:1

He giveth more grace when the burdens grow greater,
He sendeth more strength when the labors increase;
To added affliction He addeth His mercies,
To multiplied trials His multiplied peace.

His love has no limit, His grace has no measure,
His power no boundary known unto men;
For out of His infinite riches in Jesus
He giveth and giveth and giveth again.

ANNIE JOHNSON FLINT

Our prayer for today:

Our Father, we thank You that, in You, we have a loving refuge. You give to us all the love and strength we need to face the hostilities and cares of this world.

August 27

But this I say, brethren, the time is short. . . .

1 Corinthians 7:29

You who are keeping wretched quarrels alive because you cannot quite make up your mind that now is the day to sacrifice your pride and kill them;

You who are passing men sullenly upon the street, not speaking to them out of some silly spite, and yet knowing that it would fill you with shame and remorse if you heard that one of those men were dead tomorrow morning;

You who are letting your neighbor starve, till you hear that he is dying of starvation;

Or letting your friend's heart ache for a word of appreciation or sympathy, which you mean to give him someday;

If you only could know and see and feel, all of a sudden, that *"the time is short,"* how it would break the spell! How you would go instantly and do the thing which you might never have another chance to do.

PHILLIPS BROOKS

Our prayer for today:

Place in our hearts this day a conviction, Father, if there is someone we have grieved. Give us Your courage and forgiveness to amend our ways.

August 28

. . . every one that loveth is born of God, and knoweth God.

1 John 4:7

I am now deeply convinced that the power of love is from God. I believe that no one can truly love unless God is active within him. I hear Jesus say, "Without me you can do nothing. You can bear no fruit. I am the vine and you are the branches. Cut off from me you are dead." I hear St. John say that only he who knows God can know the meaning of love. I hear St. Paul describe love as the highest and greatest gift of the Spirit. Wherever I have found love I have felt the presence of God. God at work in the minds and hearts and muscles of men.

JOHN POWELL

Our prayer for today:

Teach us more of Your love, Almighty God, so that we can *really* love. May Your Holy Spirit invade our hearts, we pray.

August 29

[Love] . . . endures all things.

1 Corinthians 13:7 NAS

Real love is a very rare quality. The Bible warns that in the end times even most men's *natural* love will grow cold. Can you imagine how loudly true love speaks to a lost, dark generation? It's precisely this mysterious, wonderful, unconditional quality of the believer that will win others to Jesus. If you've been trying to witness to loved ones or an acquaintance, with little or no success, simply love them for awhile. Believe God to move upon their lives as they witness the love in you that can only be born of Him. Let them taste this spiritual fruit. Soon they'll be asking about the "tree" Himself!

PAT BOONE

Our prayer for today:

Our Savior, so often we fail to express our love to those who need You most. Sometimes we feel as if we will never reach those who are close to us. Show us any faults that are a hindrance, and fill us with Your love for others.

August 30

I will keep on expecting you to help me. . . .

Psalms 71:14 LB

In James Hilton's novel "Goodbye, Mr. Chips," the hero is a shy, inept schoolteacher, bungling and unattractive in a dozen different ways. And then something happens. He meets a woman who loves him and whom he loves, and they are married. And because of her he becomes a kind, gracious, friendly man with everyone—so much so, in fact, that he becomes the most beloved teacher in the school. There is a positive, potential power in love.

What did St. Paul mean in his great hymn to love when he said that "love does not keep a record of wrongs" (1 Corinthians 13:5 TEV)? I think he meant that to love we must be able to believe that people's characters do alter, that the leopard can change its spots, that conversions do occur, that people do repent, and that at times they do change. To put it another way, he was urging that when we are in relationships of long standing we must live in the present, not in the past.

ALAN LOY MCGINNIS

Our prayer for today:

This day is ours to share, Lord—a gift from You. The failures of yesterday are forgiven and forgotten. A hand outstretched tells how much we care for each other and for You, Lord Jesus.

August 31

> For we have not an high priest who cannot be touched with the feeling of our infirmities; but was in all points tempted like as we are, yet without sin.
>
> Hebrews 4:15

Christ, our great Good Shepherd, has Himself already gone before us into every situation and every extremity that we might encounter. We are told emphatically that He was tempted in all points like as we are. We know He entered fully and completely and very intimately into the life of men upon our planet. He has known our sufferings, experienced our sorrows, and endured our struggles in this life; He was a man of sorrows and acquainted with grief.

Because of this He *understands* us, He has totally *identified* Himself with humanity. He has, therefore, a care and compassion for us beyond our ability to grasp. No wonder He makes every possible provision to insure that when we have to cope with Satan, sin or self, the contest will not be one-sided.

W. PHILLIP KELLER

Our prayer for today:

Lord Jesus, to know You understand and have experienced the same circumstances as we have, comforts us. When we pray to You, we know You hear us and are concerned. In temptation, we will remember the power of Your name.

SEPTEMBER

September 1

But I have this against you, that you have left your first love.

Revelation 2:4 NAS

A man once came to me and told me he had just celebrated his silver wedding. He said he had been worried about his wife for the past ten years, for although he had given her so much . . . she was cold and unresponsive, and the poor man was painfully puzzled. So on their anniversary he took her out to a lovely dinner, and when she was thoroughly relaxed he plucked up courage to say to her, "Honey, we have been married twenty-five years today, and you have been a wonderful person. I want to thank you for being my wife, but for the last ten years I have been so concerned, for in spite of all the things I have given you—cars, clothes, new homes, and so on—you have been so distant and unresponsive. Please tell me why this is."

Her reply was, ". . . I am so grateful for all you have given me through the years, and I have loved everything. But, you know, for so many years you have never given me the love of your heart". . . .

It is so easy to give the Lord work, time, money, things—but how long is it since you told Jesus you love Him? Where does He come in your love life: first, second, third, or one of the also-rans?

ALAN REDPATH

Our prayer for today:

Lord Jesus Christ, forgive us for the times we do not love You as we should. May our hearts be filled with adoration for You.

September 2

> Be angry but do not sin; do not let the sun go down on your anger.
>
> Ephesians 4:26 RSV

Settle all arguments (at least to the point of agreeing to disagree) before going to bed. Too many carry the tension and frustration with them to bed and build up resentment that is not dealt with until an explosion occurs much later.

Spiritual communication is essential to oneness in marriage. It is good strategy to strive for spiritual oneness by paying attention to your mate's spirit and to your own.

TIM TIMMONS

Our prayer for today:

Lord, let us never go to sleep at night with resentments toward each other. Give us Your wisdom and love to combat any hostility, we pray.

September 3

> And when these things begin to come to pass, then look up, and lift up your heads; for your redemption draweth nigh.
>
> Luke 21:28

At the coronation of King George V and his Queen, many Americans and Canadians came over to London to see the great event. Their tickets included a seat to view the coronation procession. They were, however, greatly disappointed to discover that the seats allocated to them were on a barge on the banks of the Thames facing the Embankment wall over which they could see nothing. Many voices protested but the people were told to take refreshments in the rooms below and to wait patiently and all would be well. Meanwhile silently, but surely the tide was coming in and when ultimately the King drove past the barge was high above the wall and every eye could behold the Royal procession. We wait patiently for the coming of our King—we see Him not yet but the tide is coming in, and the waters are rising and we are lifting up our eyes in happy expectation: the signs our Lord told us to look for are being fulfilled in our midst and "at any moment."

A. LINDSAY GLEGG

Our prayer for today:

Father, our hearts are filled with joy, as we anticipate the coming of the King of kings!

September 4

The Lord is good unto them that wait for him. . . .

Lamentations 3:25

Every marriage seems to have its periods of "death" as well as "resurrection." C.S. Lewis felt this way and attributed so much divorce among Christians to their not waiting out that deadly period— the winter months of a marriage—until the spring, or resurrection, arrives.

A friend of mine likens marriage to the lilac bush in her garden. When it is bare and brittle during winter, she doesn't pull it out, only to plant a new bush each spring. Instead, she lives through that dormant period, and in the spring her lilac bush has not only grown, but it is more beautiful than ever.

Ask the Lord to help you through those periods when your marriage, your partner, and yes, yourself, are not everything they should be. Then wait for spring!

—B.B.

Our prayer for today:

We pray, our Heavenly Father, that we will be drawn near enough to You to see that only You can satisfy the deep longings in our hearts.

September 5

> As thou hast sent me into the world, even so have I also sent them
> into the world.
>
> John 17:18

To go "into the world" does not necessarily mean to travel to a
distant country or primitive tribe. "The world" is secular, godless
society; it is all round us. Christ sends us "into the world" when
He puts us into any group which does not know or honour Him. It
might be in our own street, or in an office or ship, school, hospital
or factory, or even in our own family. And here in the world we
are called to love, to serve and to offer genuine, sacrificial friendship. Paradoxically stated, the only truly Christian context in which
to witness is the world.

JOHN R. W. STOTT

Our prayer for today:

Lord, we pray today for Your missionaries all over the world.
Just as they have answered Your call, may we be ambassadors for
You wherever we find ourselves. Help us be real, compassionate
friends to those who are hurting and in need of Your forgiveness
and love!

September 6

> But the dove found no rest for the sole of her foot, and she returned
> unto him. . . . And the dove came in to him in the evening; and,
> lo, in her mouth was an olive leaf. . . .
>
> Genesis 8:9, 11

God knows just when to withhold from us any visible sign of encouragement, and when to grant us such a sign. How good it is that we may
trust Him anyway! When all visible evidences that He is remembering
us are withheld, that is best; He wants us to realize that His Word, His
promise of remembrance, is more substantial and dependable than any

evidence of our senses. When He sends the visible evidence, that is well also; we appreciate it all the more after we have trusted Him without it. Those who are readiest to trust God without other evidence than His Word always receive the greatest number of visible evidences of His love.

C. G. TRUMBULL

Our prayer for today:

Lord, even when there seems to be no sign of encouragement from You, when the days seem dark, we will *trust* You. Thank You for Your love!

September 7

As we live with Christ, our love grows more perfect and complete. . . .

1 John 4:17 LB

Married couples could enjoy each other more if they worked together more. Our foolish division of labor according to roles often leaves a wife indoors to wash the dishes while her husband goes outdoors to wash the car. Why not do both tasks together and enjoy each other's company in the process?

Part of the richness one feels in the best relationships is the result of many memories garnered over the years. Memories of favors done back and forth, tools lent, errands done, articles clipped for the other to read —a thousand tiny statements of love.

ALAN LOY MCGINNIS

Our prayer for today:

Let us find joy in the many tasks we face each day, Lord. Let the foolish barriers come down, as we find a new, deeper relationship through working side by side.

September 8

> Commit thy way unto the Lord; trust also in him; and he shall bring it to pass.

> Psalms 37:5

If your work is a burden, it is because you aren't trusting it to Him. If you do trust it to Him, you will find that the yoke He puts upon you is easy and the burden He gives you to carry is light. Even in the midst of a life of ceaseless activity, you will find rest for your soul.

If Jesus only had a band of such helpless, trusting workers, there is no limit to what He could do through them. May God raise up such an army speedily! I urge you to enlist in it and to ". . . yield your bodies to him as implements for doing right" (Romans 6:13 NEB), to be used by Him as He pleases.

> HANNAH WHITALL SMITH
> Paraphrased by
> CATHERINE JACKSON

Our prayer for today:

We need to trust You more, Lord. Teach us to commit every part of our lives to You.

September 9

> And whatever you do, do it heartily, as to the Lord, and not unto men. . . .

> Colossians 3:23

If you're a half-hearted, unreliable employee—then, you'll probably be embarrassed every time you meet your boss.

For Christians, the "boss" is God. That is why we should work with all our hearts and souls. We are answerable to the Lord for the quality of our work, and it is simply impossible to avoid meeting him: "Look," says Scripture, "the Lord is approaching, bringing rewards, to pay each man as his work deserves."

So he tells us never to be lazy or inefficient in any piece of work. No one who does his work "before the Lord" will miss his reward. Think of the angels, that vast company of heaven, spending every moment in his service, waiting instantly to obey each of his commands! "Ten thousand times ten thousand stand before him and thousands of thousands serve him, crying, "Holy, holy, holy, Lord of hosts: all creation is full of his glory."

CLEMENT OF ROME (A.D. 30–100)
Paraphrased by
DAVID WINTER

Our prayer for today:

Our Father, we would be reminded, as we go about our work, that the tasks we face are to be carried out in Your name. Nothing is too menial, nothing is too unimportant to dedicate to You, Lord.

September 10

> . . . lest any root of bitterness springing up trouble you, and thereby many be defiled.
>
> Hebrews 12:15

Sometimes when we face hard situations, we find our faith in God faltering. We feel lost and abandoned, wondering why God does not answer our prayers.

It is in these times we become, as someone once said, "bitter or better." A trite remark? Perhaps it is, on the surface, but *very* true. How we handle our heartaches and trials is watched by those around us. As we keep our faith in these dark moments and release any bitter thoughts to Him, a change takes place in our hearts, and we learn more of His unfaltering grace. Others are drawn closer to Him.

George Mueller, a man whom God used in Victorian England to establish many orphanages through simply trusting in the Lord to supply his financial needs, once said, "The only way to learn strong faith is to endure great trials. I have learned my faith by standing firm amid severe testings."

—J.W.B.

Our prayer for today:

Our Father, keep us from any bitterness when there are trials to face. May we meet them not in our strength, but in Yours.

September 11

> . . . pray to thy Father which is in secret; and thy Father which seeth in secret shall reward thee openly.
>
> Matthew 6:6

To pray is to let Jesus into our lives. He knocks and seeks admittance, not only in the solemn hours of secret prayer when you bend the knee or fold your hands in supplication, or when you hold fellowship with other Christians in a prayer meeting; nay, He knocks and seeks admittance into your life in the midst of your daily work, your daily struggles, your daily "grind." That is when you need Him most. He is always trying to come into your life, to sup with you. He sees that you need His refreshing presence most of all in the midst of your daily struggles. Listen, therefore, to Jesus as He knocks in the midst of your daily work or rest. Give heed when the Spirit beckons you to look in silent supplication to Him, who follows you day and night.

O. HALLESBY

Our prayer for today:

Lord Jesus, in the hectic pace of our lives, or in the quiet moments, may we always be aware of communing with You.

September 12

> . . . Bless me and my family forever! . . . for you, Lord God, have promised it.
>
> 2 Samuel 7:29 LB

The beautiful music of living is composed, practiced, and perfected in the harmony of home. The freedom to laugh long and loudly . . . the encouragement to participate in creative activities . . . the spontaneity of relaxed relationships that plant memories and deepen our roots in the rich, rare soil of authentic happiness. Couldn't this be included in the "all things" Paul mentioned in Romans 8:32 and 1 Timothy 6:17? The apostle tells us that our God *"richly supplies us with all things to enjoy."*

We're missing it—God's best—if the fun memories are being eclipsed by the fierce ones. The world outside the family circle is dark enough. When the light goes out *within* the circle . . . how great is the darkness.

CHARLES R. SWINDOLL

Our prayer for today:

Thank You, Lord, for our home. As we shut the door on the world and look within, at all You have provided, our hearts are grateful, indeed. Let us love and respect each other, Lord, so that the memories we are storing each day will be joyous ones.

September 13

> . . . Ask and it shall be given you; seek, and ye shall find; knock, and it shall be opened. . . .
>
> Luke 11:9

Imagine a bank safe with a gigantic door and a large combination lock on the front. This safe contains the treasures of heaven, God's safe of answers to prayer. But to open the door you have to apply the combination: "If you abide in Me," and turn the big wheel until it clicks, "and My words abide in you," we turn it in the opposite direction until it clicks, "ask whatever you wish," and again turn the combination wheel until it clicks, "and it shall be done for you." Now just take hold of the gigantic handle and open the door. Inside the safe are all of God's good things which are available to us if we simply apply that combination.

By His example and teaching, Jesus encourages us to ask God for specific requests—those which have to do with our needs, our relationships, or anything that concerns us.

VONETTE Z. BRIGHT

Our prayer for today:

Lord Jesus, in Your name, today we are able to come with our requests. We search our hearts to see whether we are really abiding in You, so that we are assured of an answer.

September 14

For if you give, you will get! Your gift will return to you in full and overflowing measure, pressed down, shaken together to make room for more, and running over. . . .

Luke 6:38 LB

The Bible looks upon marriage not as a social contract between two individuals that may be dissolved at will; rather it looks upon marriage as a mystery. St. Paul, writing to the Ephesians, says, "For this reason a man shall leave his father and mother and be joined to his wife and the two shall become one." Then he goes on and says, "This is a great mystery, and I take it to mean Christ and the Church" (Ephesians 5:31–32). In other words, your marriage—every Christian marriage— is designed to be a reflection of the relationship between Christ and His Church.

Thus, contrary to natural thinking, much of the real joy in marriage comes from *giving,* not *getting.* For marriage is modeled on the relationship between Christ and His Church.

LARRY CHRISTENSON

Our prayer for today:

Lord Jesus, teach us to give to each other, as You gave Your love and life. May we look for opportunities each day to show how much we care.

September 15

Now the God of hope fill you with all joy and peace in believing, that ye may abound in hope, through the power of the Holy Ghost.

Romans 15:13

Hope at its deepest is not focused on particulars. At its core hope looks *beyond* a cure for disease, a solution for a problem, an escape from pain, for assurance from God that life has point and meaning in spite of disease, problems, and pain. Hope looks to the promise of the final victory of Jesus Christ over all that hurts and kills. This is the hope that gives a person courage to praise today and to face tomorrow with expectancy even when one does not expect the problem to be solved. Love breeds this hope in both the person loved and the loving person.

LEWIS B. SMEDES

Our prayer for today:

Lord Jesus, fill us with the hope of Your victory, so that we can face all our problems positively. As we rely completely on You, we shall be filled with You and peace.

September 16

When thou saidst, Seek ye my face; my heart said unto thee, Thy face, Lord, will I seek.

Psalms 27:8

A sense of being able to talk to somebody, or of expressing adulation and gratefulness through ordinary, everyday acts. And a growing conviction that while it is good and right to go to a formal place of worship, it is even more important to worship God wherever we are. All altars are not confined to churches. Your altar may be your desk, the machine you operate, the kitchen stove. The Lord of Life may be known and adored through any deed that we dedicate to him and to the benefit of other people, whether that deed be typing a letter, turning out shoes, or making a family's dinner.

MARJORIE HOLMES

Our prayer for today:

Everywhere we go, whatever circumstances we find ourselves in, let our lives reflect Your example, Lord Jesus.

September 17

. . . love goes on forever. . . .

1 Corinthians 13:8 LB

The other day Bill came to take me to lunch. . . . While we were waiting for our food, a teacher Bill had had in grade school came in with her husband. Bill had talked of her often—her love of learning, her energy and enthusiasm for teaching. . . . But this day she came in very slowly, holding to her husband's arm. She had been stricken by a stroke some months before. . . . There was such gentleness in the way her husband pulled out her chair and took her coat. The way he looked at her told us that there was something he was seeing that went beyond the face wearied and pale from long days of suffering. He reached across the table and tenderly untied her bandana, lovingly patting her cheek as he did so. He then unfolded her napkin and helped her to order. Everything about the way he looked at her and held her hand declared that she was his princess and he was her adoring knight.

The disinterested passerby might have seen only an elderly couple, past the prime of life by Hollywood standards, and certainly incapable of romance. But what does Hollywood know? There was something in the way these two people related to each other that made us know that somewhere—far back down the road—two lovers, perhaps then young and beautiful, had made a commitment to each other. Somewhere they had joined their hands before an altar and repeated those familiar words—"To love and to cherish, 'til death us do part."

They had meant it. They had loved each other, invested in each other, and the two had "become one flesh." And as a result—their love had grown to be *real.*

Bill reached for my hand across the table. We bowed our heads silently. I knew he was praying, as I was:

"Lord, make our love grow like that. May our commitment to each be *real.* Let us always see each other through love's eyes."

GLORIA GAITHER

September 18

> But if ye do not forgive, neither will your Father which is in heaven forgive your trespasses.
>
> Mark 11:26

A disciple asked Jesus how often one should forgive an offender; seven times? The reply was if someone offended you, tell him (let him know calmly, objectively, if possible, but at any rate let him know) that he has been hitting below the belt. If he repents, forgive him, not seven times but seventy times seven.

What happens if the offender doesn't repent? You forgive anyway. Christ further taught that forgiveness does not depend upon the repentance of the offender. He taught that if anyone offends, you are to forgive the offender the next time you come to pray.

DOUGLAS ROBERTS

Our prayer for today:

It is so hard, Lord, to forgive the slights and hurts that seem so unjustified. Yet, we remember how many times we have hurt You. Forgive us, Lord. Pour into our hearts Your divine forgiveness for those who offend us.

September 19

I will not leave you comfortless. . . .

John 14:18

Christ does not leave us comfortless, but we have
to be in dire need of comfort to know the truth of His promise.
It is in times of calamity . . .
   in days and nights of sorrow and trouble
    that the presence
     the sufficiency
       and the sympathy of God grow very sure
       and very wonderful.
Then we find out that the grace of God is sufficient
for all our needs
   for every problem
    and for every difficulty
for every broken heart, and for every human sorrow.
   It is in times of bereavement that one begins to understand the
meaning of immortality.

PETER MARSHALL

Our prayer for today:

We have felt Your comfort, Lord, and it has sustained us. In days
of sorrow, we learn more of Your abiding grace. Thank You for healing
our brokenness.

September 20 .

A man . . . shall cleave unto his wife. . . .

Genesis 2:24

This means that his wife has his primary consideration at all times.
A man is not to love his parents any less, but he is not to allow them
to meddle in his family life. Your wife has first consideration. "You
mean my wife merits more consideration than my parents?" Yes! Your

parents are to be loved and respected and obeyed, but your wife is your first consideration in God's sight. When you took her you entered into the closest relationship in human life, the relationship of husband and wife.

I want to tell husbands this—we cannot be the right kind of husbands or fathers without Jesus Christ. We don't have the strength or capacity, we cannot live up to the Christian ideal of marriage, until we yield our lives to Christ.

BILLY GRAHAM

Our prayer for today:

Dear Father, thank You for our parents, whom we do not love less because of our marriage. But in all decisions now, Lord, we ask that we will rightfully put each other first, as we consider each other's welfare.

September 21

Marriage is honourable in all, and the bed undefiled. . . .

Hebrews 13:4

The whole idea of husbands and wives as partners who are created to meet each other's needs is evident in the verse, "Then the Lord said, 'It is not good for the man to be alone. I will provide a partner for him' " (Genesis 2:18). The creation story indicates that our maleness and femaleness come from God and that God gave his blessing to the couple with instructions to "be fruitful and increase" (Genesis 1:27, 28). So the story of man's beginnings in the Bible has the basic couple entering into a sexual relationship from which came children. This is why sex ought not to be something to be embarrassed or ashamed about.

KENNETH CHAFIN

Our prayer for today:

Lord, how beautiful is the gift of sex. In it, we find a relationship that is meant only for each other. Together we thank You, our Father.

September 22

> . . . let every man be swift to hear. . . .

James 1:19

Husbands and wives call out to each other from *a need to be loved* and *a need to love.* The loving partner answers initially by listening to that call, understanding it, and responding to it. Listening love is willing to receive love as well; so listening love is a first evidence that husband and wife are free to make a full response to one another.

Jesus loved through listening. No one ever listened as Jesus did; neither has any other one exhibited greater love than He. The inseparable nature of loving and listening is exemplified most beautifully and uniquely in our Lord.

DWIGHT HERVEY SMALL

Our prayer for today:

Jesus, You always took time to listen. Help us to really respond to each other's needs, giving our full attention and really hearing the other's heart cry.

September 23

> But we all, with open face beholding as in a glass the glory of the Lord, are changed into the same image from glory to glory even as by the Spirit of the Lord.

2 Corinthians 3:18

We try to change people to conform to our ideas of how they should be. So does God. But there the similarity ends. Our ideas of what the other person should do or how he should act may be an improvement or an imprisonment. We may be setting the other person free of behavior patterns that are restricting his development, or we may be simply chaining him up in another behavioral bondage. So even with the best of motives our attempts to change others brings us into an area "where angels fear to tread." Yet tread we must! And we tread with safety only as we walk in the love and mercy and justice of God.

JAMES FAIRFIELD

Our prayer for today:

Father, we pray that we might not stand in Your way by trying to change each other. May our lives be so transparent that the changes necessary will be made by Your Holy Spirit.

September 24

> Great peace have they which love thy law: and nothing shall offend them.
>
> Psalms 119:165

What a motivation to get into the Word of God and find out what God wants to say to us. Our approach to the Bible should be like listening to a *voice* rather than reading a book. We should hear His voice saying, "This is your Father speaking. Listen!" If He has taken the trouble to put into writing the thoughts, ideas, and words He wants to communicate to us, He wants to be listened to and obeyed. When God speaks, He means to be taken seriously.

It takes three people to make a lasting marriage—a man, a woman, and God. Our communication link to each other as husband and wife has to be forged stronger as the years go by. Even more vital is our communication link individually with the One who created us both.

JACK and CAROLE MAYHALL

Our prayer for today:

Dear God, give us a deeper love for Your Word, so that we may be able to communicate, not only with each other, but in a stronger, more positive way with You, Lord.

September 25

> . . . don't be troubled or afraid.

> John 14:27 LB

Lillian Dickson and her husband felt called by God to the island called Formosa. When they arrived, they talked to a government official in Social Services. He looked at this young and naive couple and laughed, "Look, go back to America. You can't possibly succeed here. There is no way!"

He stood up and walked over to the window and pointed outside. "Look, you can see the ocean. Helping people here in Formosa is like trying to change the ocean one bucket at a time!"

Young Lillian Dickson got out her chair and said, "Well, then I am going to fill my bucket!" And they left the room. Fifty plus years later, her husband dead, Lillian is still filling her bucket. She has established over one thousand churches, schools and hospitals. It all happened because she and her husband had the courage and the willingness to fail!

If they had turned around and gone home, no one would have blamed them. But they stayed and faced possible futility. And Formosa is a better place today because of their courage!

ROBERT H. SCHULLER

Our prayer for today:

Thank You, our Father, for the example of the saints, whose lives reflect Your courage. Show us where we should serve You, and give us brave hearts to honor You.

September 26

> . . . Inasmuch as ye have done it unto one of the least of these my brethren, ye have done it unto me.

> Matthew 25:40

There are many who want me to tell them of secret ways of becoming perfect and I can only tell them that the sole secret is a hearty love of

God, and the only way of attaining that love is by loving. You learn to speak by speaking, to study by studying, to run by running, to work by working; and just so you learn to love God and man by loving. Begin as a mere apprentice and the very power of love will lead you on to become a master of the art.

FRANCIS DE SALES

Our prayer for today:

Father, we stumble and fall so many times, as we try to learn the real meaning of love. May two apprentices ask You for the power of Your love in their lives? Thank You, our Lord and God.

September 27

> . . . In the world ye shall have tribulation: but be of good cheer;
> I have overcome the world.

John 16:33

If you care nothing for your own life, if you have no dreams and goals and high purposes, then you cannot be defeated. You have surrendered the game before it even started. Let us take defeat as a badge of greatness. The fact that you have been defeated indicates something high and holy and good about you. It was soldier-writer Donald Hankey who said that "Religion is betting one's life there is a God." When you really make that commitment, then you begin to believe in all the high and holy purposes in life. As you believe, you begin to commit yourself, and your life begins to take on meaning and purpose. Then it is that you can be hurt and thwarted and even defeated. I would hate to admit to the fact that I had escaped defeat in life. Sure, defeat is not easy to bear, but an athletic team would never be defeated, if they never went out on the field to play the game. A person will never be defeated who never tries to do anything, or amount to anything. Be glad for your defeats. Quit crying about them. Start shouting praises for them. Without defeats you are nothing.

CHARLES L. ALLEN

Our prayer for today:

Thank You, our Father, that in defeat we can learn more of Your faithfulness and goodness. By Your grace and comfort, we rise up and praise You. Let there be no bitterness, only deeper love for You.

September 28

. . . so shall we ever be with the Lord. Wherefore comfort one another with these words.

1 Thessalonians 4:17, 18

I remember the day I received a cable informing me my father had suddenly died. When the stark reality of his death hit me, I sat down on my bed and cried inconsolably. Then I felt Bill's arms around me. I looked up and saw tears in his eyes, for he was feeling my hurt, too. Can there be any description that could adequately express my thankfulness to the Lord for having someone care so deeply when I hurt?

There are many times in our lives when we need comfort. It does not always have to be something so overwhelming as the loss of a loved one. There are times of failure, times of disappointment, times when just nothing seems to go right.

It is then that just a word, a touch, or an arm around a shoulder tells you so much. With renewed spirits, we can face the world, knowing we are loved by another person and our Lord Jesus Christ.

—J.W.B.

Our prayer for today:

Dear Lord, keep our hearts and minds so at one with You that when either of us hurts we can respond, showing we care and understand.

September 29

My brethren, count it all joy when ye fall into divers temptations; Knowing this, that the trying of your faith worketh patience.

James 1:2,3

Disappointments and trouble are often the instruments with which we are fashioned for better and bigger things to come. You must never give up. Life never takes away from us without giving something better in its place. Life is no straight and easy corridor; the road is not always smooth and unhampered. Many times our paths are like a maze of passages through which we must seek, search, and find our way. At times we find our way and then are confused—now a clear light to go, then checked by a red light to stop. At one time we find ourselves on a freeway and then again in a blind alley. But always—if we have faith —God will open another door. Perhaps not the door we thought was the best, but another door which He knows is the best, will take us to a greater and more useful destination. Out of my deepest hurts have come my greatest strength.

DON H. POLSTON

Our prayer for today:

Father, from the hurts of life may we learn the enormity of Your love. In disappointments, we will find a better way—in sorrow, comfort for our tears and a strength that can only come from Your grace and power.

September 30

Even so it is not the will of your Father which is in heaven, that one of these little ones should perish.

Matthew 18:14

"That the children might not be as their fathers, a generation that set not their heart aright, and whose spirit was not steadfast with God" —Psalms 78:8.

"I will pour My Spirit upon thy seed, and My blessing upon thy offspring"—Isaiah 44:3.

Pray for the rising generation, who are to come after us. Think of the young men and young women and children of this age, and pray for all the agencies at work among them; that in associations and societies and unions, in homes and schools, Christ may be honoured, and the

Holy Spirit get possession of them. Pray for the young of your own neighbourhood.

ANDREW MURRAY

Our prayer for today:

Give us hearts of love for the younger generation, Father. We have experienced the hurts and challenges of life. Now they, too, will face the bewilderment of a changing, hostile world. May they know the comfort, wisdom, and peace that comes from knowing Your Son, Jesus Christ.

OCTOBER

October 1

For with God nothing shall be impossible.

Luke 1:37

You cannot plan a budget and expect God to direct your steps, until you are willing to honor Him with the firstfruits of your income. In other words, obey God and plan your tithe the very first thing. " 'Bring the whole tithe into the storehouse, so that there may be food in My house, and test Me now in this,' says the Lord of hosts, 'if I will not open for you the windows of heaven, and pour out for you a blessing until there is no more need' " (Malachi 3:10 NAS). Now *there* is a promise that you cannot afford to pass up. The Lord says to test Him by giving the whole tithe to Him—and He will bless you until there is no more need. It sounds impossible, but remember that our God deals in the impossible things of life and He challenges you to test Him.

TIM and BEV LAHAYE

Our prayer for today:

The human in us says, "We can't afford to give You the firstfruits, Lord!" The quiet voice that comes from You assures us You will bless our tithe and take care of all our needs. Help us give You, from thankful hearts, that which is rightfully Yours.

218

October 2

> . . . Behold, like the clay in the potter's hand, so are you in my hand. . . .
>
> Jeremiah 18:6 RSV

I loved that period of time when our two sons were learning to walk. They would do so well for a couple of steps, and then—crash—down to the floor they would go. It would usually hurt a little, but looking up to Joan or me, they would reach out their hands so we could lift them up and get them started once more.

For some couples, marriage is like that. For a while, all goes well, but before long the relationship begins to go off balance. There doesn't seem to be progress, and the marriage doesn't seem to go anywhere. Eventually they give up trying.

Oliver Goldsmith, an English playwright, once said, "Our greatest glory consists not in never falling, but in rising every time we fall."

During those times of need in your marriage, reach out in trust to the One who said, "Come unto me," allowing His grace and strength to guide your steps together.

—B.B.

Our prayer for today:

Lord, teach us how to receive Your guidance. Make us aware of Your gentle direction in our lives.

October 3

> As they continued their journey, Jesus came to a village and a woman called Martha welcomed him to her house. She had a sister by the name of Mary who settled down at the Lord's feet and was listening to what he said. But Martha was very worried about her elaborate preparations and she burst in, saying,
>
> "Lord, don't you mind that my sister has left me to do everything by myself? Tell her to come and help me!"
>
> But the Lord answered her,

"Martha, my dear, you are worried and bothered about providing so many things. Only one thing is really needed. Mary has chosen the best part and it must not be taken away from her!"

. . .

Now Jesus loved Martha and her sister and Lazarus.

Luke 10:38–42; John 11:5 PHILLIPS

It happened in a home—and that is the significance of this story.

There was this beautiful home in Bethany where Jesus loved to come and rest. After tiring days in Jerusalem—teaching, answering questions, being opposed by the leaders—He would walk the two miles to Bethany to spend the evening there and rest.

In the Bethany home, Jesus found peace. Your life and mine are meant to be a Bethany—a place of rest for Him.

FESTO KIVENGERE

Our prayer for today:

Our hearts are grateful, Lord Jesus, for our home. When we become encumbered with our daily routine, help us to remember You are present—always willing to give Your perfect peace.

October 4

Wherefore by their fruits ye shall know them.

Matthew 7:20

All good home life tends inevitably towards the practice of the Christian virtues. Indeed, it is only in terms of those virtues that family living can be successful at all. Every truly happy home, therefore, whether it professes to be a Christian home or not, is Christian in spirit.

The distinctive mark of a Christian home is that it is Christian both in its spirit and in its profession. It is necessary that it should be both of these. Christian virtues, as we have seen, can be cultivated by people who do not acknowledge the Christian faith. It is equally true that people may profess and call themselves Christians who have not the spirit of Christ. It is a sad state of affairs indeed when a home which calls itself Christian does not manifest the fruits of Christian living.

DAVID R. MACE

Our prayer for today:

Does our home shine with Christian love, Lord? How much we fail to give love to each other and to those around us. We pray that Your Holy Spirit will fill our hearts and our house.

October 5

> . . . he which made them at the beginning made them male and female . . . and they twain shall be one flesh.

Matthew 19:4,5

God made Adam and Eve as two very different people who could become one unit. Male and female created He them—on purpose. God made woman to be physically beautiful in the eyes of man. God also made man to be beautiful in the eyes of the woman. Two kinds of beauty, complementing each other, fulfilling each other. God gave man and woman capacity for love and someone to love, capacity for gentleness and someone to whom to be gentle, capacity for communication and someone with whom to communicate, capacity for worshiping Him and having communication with Him—their God—and someone with whom to join for worship, capacity for learning and someone with whom to discuss all the new discoveries and understandings, capacity for physical oneness and someone with whom to become one in a mysterious and very real way.

EDITH SCHAEFFER

Our prayer for today:

Thank You, our Father, for bringing us together, for making us one, so that we can share the beauty of life with You.

October 6

> For he knoweth our frame; he remembereth that we are dust.
>
> Psalms 103:14

True love always carries a risk with it, on a human level. If we are to be honest and open and give of ourselves, we risk the possibility of being hurt. We are imperfect beings—so are our mates—and, eventually, we are going to hurt each other, either inadvertently or purposely.

What does the Bible say about the fear of being hurt? "God has not given us a spirit of fear, but of power and of love and of a sound mind" (2 Timothy 1:7). It also says that God binds the wounds of the brokenhearted (*see* Psalms 147:3), so we won't be permanently disabled by crushed feelings. Our problems come from expecting too much of our mates. No one except God is completely dependable and our world needn't fall apart when our partner lets us down in one instance. There will undoubtedly be times when we let him down, too. Don't think of it as rejection—think of it as human failing. Then forgive and forget.

LOU BEARDSLEY

Our prayer for today:

Sometimes, Lord, we do hurt each other, and our feelings are bruised. Help us to see, through these experiences, that we are often insensitive to the other's needs. Heal our wounds and fill our hearts with Your forgiving love.

October 7

> It is plain to anyone with eyes to see that at the present time all created life groans in a sort of universal travail. And it is plain, too, that we who have a foretaste of the Spirit are in a state of painful tensions, while we wait for that redemption of our bodies which will mean that we have realised our full sonship in him.
>
> Romans 8:18–23 PHILLIPS

Looking back across the years of my life, I can see the working of a divine pattern which is the way of God with His children. When I was in a prison camp in Holland during the war, I often prayed, "Lord, never let the enemy put me in a German concentration camp." God answered *no* to that prayer. Yet in the German camp, with all its horror, I found many prisoners who had never heard of Jesus Christ. If God had not used my sister Betsie and me to bring them to Him, they would never have heard of Him. Many died, or were killed, but many died with the name of Jesus on their lips. They were well worth all our suffering. Faith is like radar which sees through the fog—the reality of things at a distance that the human eye cannot see.

CORRIE TEN BOOM

Our prayer for today:

Our Father, in the pattern of our lives, we see Your divine leading. Through any suffering, You are there. In faith, we know we can be sustained and used to bring others to Your Son, Jesus Christ.

October 8

Ye have heard that it hath been said, Thou shalt love thy neighbour, and hate thine enemy. But I say unto you, Love your enemies. . . .

Matthew 5:43,44

Christ turned the world's accepted standards upside down. It was the poor, not the rich, who were blessed; the weak, not the strong, who were to be esteemed; the pure in heart, not the sophisticated and the worldly, who understood what life was about. Righteousness, not power or money or sensual pleasure, should be man's pursuit. We should love our enemies, bless them that curse us, do good to them that hate us, and pray for them that despitefully use us, in order that we may be worthy members of a human family whose father is in heaven.

MALCOLM MUGGERIDGE

Our prayer for today:

Lord Jesus, without Your love we cannot love as we should; we cannot forgive or live according to Your standards. Take away the obstacles in our lives that keep us from being filled with Your love. We ask this in Your beloved name.

October 9

> Judge not, that ye be not judged. For with what judgment ye judge,
> ye shall be judged. . . .
>
> Matthew 7:1,2

The counsel of Jesus is to abstain from judging. This sounds strange at first because the characteristic of the Holy Spirit is to reveal things that are wrong, but the strangeness is only on the surface. The Holy Spirit does reveal what is wrong in others, but His discernment is never for purposes of criticism, but for purposes of intercession. When the Holy Spirit reveals something of the nature of sin and unbelief in another, His purpose is not to make us feel smug satisfaction, but to make us lay hold of God for that one, asking God to help him overcome that evil way. Never ask God for discernment, for discernment increases your responsibility. Simply bring that one before God until God puts him right.

OSWALD CHAMBERS

Our prayer for today:

Father, how easy it is to judge and criticize. When we see another's faults, help us to bring that one to You, lovingly, in prayer.

October 10

> The Lord is merciful and gracious, slow to anger, and plenteous
> in mercy. He will not always chide: neither will he keep his anger
> for ever.
>
> Psalms 103:8,9

Conflict is a dimension of companionship. Who said that companionship always implied that the waters of relationship would be smooth? The fact is, if there is going to be any viable sharing of minds in a relationship, there will be moments when issues and perspectives are going to be fine-tuned to such an extent that disagreement will be raised. Conflict is the evidence that there is some distance between the viewpoints of two partners.

Many Christians have felt that having conflict is unspiritual—that it indicates that a relationship is in trouble. On a few occasions I have met couples who claimed that they had never had a conflict. I am always reminded of the statement Dr. Leslie Weatherhead once made about such couples and which Paul Tournier quotes: "Either these people are lying, or one of them has crushed the other."

GORDON MACDONALD

Our prayer for today:

Father, often our days are not abounding with calm and agreement. Thank You, Lord, that we can come to You and seek Your wisdom. Let us give each other the courtesy of expressing our feelings honestly, so we may grow.

October 11

> To them who by patient continuance in well doing seek for glory and honour and immortality, [will God give] eternal life.
>
> Romans 2:7

Most people, if they had really learned to look into their own hearts, would know that they do want, and want acutely, something that cannot be had in this world. There are all sorts of things in this world that offer to give it to you, but they never quite keep their promise. The longings which arise in us when we first fall in love, or first think of some foreign country, or first take up some subject that excites us, are longings which no marriage, no travel, no learning, can really satisfy. I am not now speaking of what would ordinarily be called unsuccessful marriages, or holidays, or learned careers. I am speaking of the best possible ones. There was something we grasped at, in that first moment of longing, which just fades away in reality. I think everyone knows what I mean. The wife may be a good wife, and the hotels and scenery may have been excellent, and chemistry may be a very interesting job: but something has evaded us.

C. S. LEWIS

Our prayer for today:

It is Your presence in our marriage, Lord Jesus, that provides the answer to all our longings!

October 12

For the Lord shall be thy confidence. . . .

Proverbs 3:26

Belief in each other is so important in marriage. We can fail miserably in the world, our day can be *ghastly* in every way, but when we return home, a word, a sign of love, can help ease the pain of defeat. We have the confidence of our loved one.

When President Theodore Roosevelt reflected on his possible defeat at the next election, he said, "No matter what happened, my happiness was assured—for my life with Edith and my children constitutes my happiness." He knew his wife believed in him, whatever the result.

Success depends largely on our belief in each other. Anne Morrow Lindbergh, remembering her future husband's part in helping her career, said, "The man I was to marry believed in me and what I could do, and consequently I found I could do more than I realized."

We can all do more than we realize, if we know that someone thinks of us as a worthy individual. Jesus Christ did just that, when He died on the Cross, signifying that each of us is worthy of His love. Realizing this, we can transmit to each other a believing, encouraging love that encompasses and consoles. We can face the world!

—J.W.B.

Our prayer for today:

Lord, help us to show how much we love and believe in each other. Thank You, Lord, for Your love, which assures us that we are esteemed by You.

October 13

. . . being knit together in love. . . .

Colossians 2:2

Thousands of couples go through with a loveless marriage because no one ever told them what genuine love is. . . . I believe we need to read the 13th chapter of First Corinthians, in which the Apostle Paul gives us a definition of love. He says, "Love is patient and kind; love is not jealous or boastful; it is not arrogant or rude. Love does not insist on its own way; it is not irritable or resentful; it does not rejoice at wrong, but rejoices in the right. Love bears all things, believes all things, hopes all things, endures all things. Love never ends." If people today knew that kind of love, the divorce rate would be sharply reduced.

BILLY GRAHAM

Our prayer for today:

Help us, Lord, to remember the attributes of real love. We will face pressures, but let us remember that Your love is in our hearts. The knowledge of this will help us transcend our problems.

October 14

Simon, Simon, Satan has asked to have you, to sift you like wheat, but I have pleaded in prayer for you. . . .

Luke 22:31, 32 LB

Jesus prayed for Peter! And in praying for Peter, Jesus still saw possibilities in Peter, though he was weak and undependable. . . .

Gutzon Borglum, the sculptor who carved the famous bust of Lincoln, had a cleaning woman who dusted the block of marble from which the great carving was sculpted. To the cleaning woman, the chunk of marble was simply one of the many shapeless blocks amidst the clutter. One day, after Borglum had started sculpturing the block, chipping until the unmistakable profile of Lincoln began to emerge, the cleaning woman studied the block, then rushed to Borglum's secretary, asking, "Ain't that Abraham Lincoln?" When told it was, she exclaimed, "Well, how in the world did Mr. Borglum know that Lincoln was in that piece of marble?"

How did Jesus know that an apostle was in that fickle fisherman, Peter? He knew through praying. How may you know that a disciple is in that block of flesh which is your friend, who is slipping? Again, you know through praying.

WILLIAM P. BARKER

Our prayer for today:

Jesus, keep us from judging the outer shell, and help us see, with Your eyes, the beauty of another's soul.

October 15

If ye keep my commandments; ye shall abide in my love; even as I have kept my Father's commandments, and abide in his love. . . . This is my commandment, That ye love one another, as I have loved you.

John 15:10, 12

Jesus came to fulfill every command, and having loved His own, He loved them to the end, and thus all the requirements of His law were met by His life, because His every motive was love. He did not set aside any of the Commandments. He established them all that in the mighty force of His love to the heart of His people He would set up His kingdom of love in them by His Holy Spirit.

ALAN REDPATH

Our prayer for today:

Lord, may our lives be so yielded to You that they will radiate the love that only Your Holy Spirit can inspire.

October 16

> Never pay back evil for evil. Let your aims be such as all men count honourable. If possible, so far as it lies with you, live at peace with all men.

> Romans 12:17, 18 NEB

But how do we give up this need to hurt back? Paul is very clear in Ephesians 4 on how this can be done. After reminding us in verse 26 about anger's potential for leading us into sin, he proceeds to say: "Have done with spite and passion, all angry shouting and cursing, and bad feeling of every kind. Be generous to one another, tender-hearted, *forgiving* one another as God in Christ forgave you" (vv. 31, 32 NEB; italics added).

Forgiveness is the key to giving up your need to hurt back, and the genius of Christianity is in the fact that forgiveness of others is made possible through God's forgiveness of us.

ARCHIBALD D. HART

Our prayer for today:

May we keep our eyes on You, our gentle Savior, who, when enduring the most despicable treatment, prayed for those who ill-treated You. Make us tenderhearted and forgiving, Lord Jesus.

October 17

> . . . but then shall I know even as also I am known.

> 1 Corinthians 13:12

When we strip ourselves of our masks and allow ourselves to be known fully, the sexual experience can be immeasurably heightened. You invite the other to know you sexually and your mate invites you to know him or her sexually. Sex ought to be an expression of the joy of life, a sharing of the good things in life. Sex that is deeply enjoyed is freely given and taken, with deep, soul-shaking climaxes, and makes a well-married couple look at each other from time to time and wink and grin. We become humble at the remembrance of joys past and expectant of those yet to be enjoyed.

ALAN LOY MCGINNIS

Our prayer for today:

Thank You, Lord, for these times spent together, which are completely our own! Help us to express to each other the joy and love we experience.

October 18

Though he slay me, yet will I trust in him. . . .

Job 13:15

Bad experiences—major life problems, tragic circumstances, or painful trials—have often destroyed what had *seemed* to be a strong faith in God. In fact, those whose faith is based on the experiences which happen to them are certainly destined to lose that faith, because very certainly some misfortune will strike them. God has never promised us a rose garden. Instead He has promised us that "in this world ye *shall* have tribulation." Unless we live in some kind of emotional Disneyland, troubles and tribulations will come our way, and if we—like Job's friends—believe that the righteous shall not suffer, then we are surely to be faced eventually with having to blame God or ourselves.

CONSTANCE P. THARP

Our prayer for today:

Our faith wavers sometimes, Lord. It seems when trouble descends on us, it is easy to question, "Why?" But we will remember Job and those saints whose lives in tribulation have glorified You.

October 19

> . . . doing service, as to the Lord. . . .

Ephesians 6:7

Once you have taken the step of faith by which you put yourself wholly and absolutely into God's hands, you must expect Him to begin to work. His way of accomplishing what you have entrusted to Him may be different from what you had in mind. But you must rest in the assurance that He knows what He is doing.

Flora entered into this life of faith with a great outpouring of the Spirit and a wonderful flood of light and joy. Thinking that this was a preparation for some great service, she expected to be led at once into a public ministry. Instead, her husband almost immediately suffered a severe business loss, and she had to stay at home and manage a large and busy household. She had no time or energy left for any activities outside of her home. Accepting the discipline, she swept, dusted, baked, and sewed with as much devotion as she would have preached, taught, or written for the Lord. Through this period of training, God was able to make her into a ". . . vessel for noble use . . . ready for any good work" (2 Timothy 2:21 RSV).

HANNAH WHITALL SMITH
Paraphrased by
CATHERINE JACKSON

Our prayer for today:

Jesus, in all our work here on earth, may we constantly remember that no service is so menial that it cannot bring joy as we do it in Your name.

October 20

> So encourage each other to build each other up, just as you are already doing.

1 Thessalonians 5:11 LB

Let the husband love, pursue, and remember his wife and she will, out of the overflow of her heart, praise and exalt him. If I understand the Scriptures correctly, the wife should be the reflection of the husband as the church is the reflection of her Lord. Praise glorifies the Lord, and compliments will build the image of the home. Your self-image will usually not be any greater than the image which you receive from your husband or wife. Compliment without a thought of reward, and watch the rewards come pouring back into your life!

I don't know any conflicts in the home that cannot be cured by sincere compliments. Compliments can heal your home.

DON H. POLSTON

Our prayer for today:

Father, help us to encourage each other. Sensitize our hearts, so that we will be able to sincerely appreciate and love as we should.

October 21

In whom are hid all the treasures of wisdom and knowledge.

Colossians 2:3

Only God can steer the course of your life with divine discretion because *He* knows what *He* is doing. He is able to declare the end from the beginning to you. You have trusted Him to forgive and forget your past, and you expect Him to deliver you safely in heaven. Therefore, you *must* give Him the right to prove Himself to be as capable of organizing and directing in *time,* as you know and expect Him to be adequate for *eternity.* You have a throne room, which is His by right —is He at home sitting on His throne, ruling and reigning and signing the decrees? This is your responsibility to provide the King with a home fit for a King!

D. STUART BRISCOE

Our prayer for today:

Father, may we search our hearts this day and see where we fail to make You King of our lives and home.

October 22

> These things I have spoken unto you, that in me ye might have peace. In the world ye shall have tribulation: but be of good cheer; I have overcome the world.

John 16:33

Peace is the spirit and soul of persons so imbued with the presence of God's Gracious Spirit that they are not easily provoked: They are not "touchy." They are not irritable or easily enraged. Their pride is not readily pricked. They do not live like a bristling porcupine with all its quills extended in agitated self-defense.

Peace is actually the exact opposite. It is the quiet, potent, gracious attitude of serenity and good-will that comes to meet the onslaught of others with good cheer, equanimity, and strong repose.

To see and understand this quality of life at its best we simply must turn away from our contemporaries and look at Christ . . . God very God.

W. PHILLIP KELLER

Our prayer for today:

Keep our eyes on You, Lord Jesus, our source of peace. Forgive us when we become touchy with each other and our home is far from the peaceful place we know it should be.

October 23

> . . . in quietness and in confidence shall be your strength. . . .

Isaiah 30:15

The psychologists tell us that if two people are going to communicate with each other they have to have confidence in each other. Now confidence is simply a synonym for the good old biblical word *faith.* In Colossians 2:6 we are told, "As ye have therefore received Christ Jesus the Lord, so walk ye in him." How did you receive Jesus Christ? By faith. By putting your faith and confidence in what He has done to save you. We are to live our Christian life moment by moment by the same principle. In Galatians 2:20 we read, "I am crucified with Christ: nevertheless I live; yet not I, but Christ liveth in me: and the life which I now live in the flesh I live by the faith of the Son of God, who loved me, and gave himself for me." This is learning to rely moment by moment in Jesus Christ and His power within us.

CURTIS C. MITCHELL

Our prayer for today:

Lord, may we rely completely on Your power to direct us, as we grow closer together. In the quietness of our beings, we find Your strength, Lord Jesus.

October 24

> ... pray for us unto the Lord thy God. ... That the Lord thy God may shew us the way wherein we may walk, and the thing that we may do.
>
> Jeremiah 42:2, 3

We can't choose happiness either for ourselves or for another; we can't tell where that will lie. We can only choose whether we will indulge ourselves in the present moment, or whether we will renounce that, for the sake of obeying the Divine voice within us—for the sake of being true to all the motives that sanctify our lives. I know this belief is hard; it has slipped away from me again and again; but I have felt that if I let it go forever, I should have no light through the darkness of this life.

GEORGE ELIOT

Our prayer for today:

Lord God, our attempts to bring happiness into our lives are futile, if You are not leading us. May we be obedient to Your will, so that Your joy will fill our hearts and the hearts of those around us.

October 25

> . . . as Christ loved the church and gave himself up for her. . . .

Ephesians 5:25 RSV

At first glance one sees the husband and father set as authority over his wife and children, and this seems like a fine perch for the man: "I'm the lord of my castle, the sovereign, the liege." . . . But one must look deeper. For the divine authority vested in a husband and father is modeled upon Christ. And Christ's authority was rooted in the sacrifice of Himself. Only when Calvary was behind Him did He come to His disciples and say, "All authority in heaven and on earth has been given to me" (Matthew 28:18). The authority of Christ, and therefore the authority of a husband and father, is not a human, "fleshy" authority. It is not one person lording it over others. *It is a divine and spiritual authority which is rooted in the sacrifice of one's self.*

LARRY CHRISTENSON

Our prayer for today:

Lord Jesus, teach us our rightful roles, so that our marriage will glorify You.

October 26

> . . . weep with them that weep.

Romans 12:15

Let us try, all of us, to come closer to that unity of spreading Christ's love wherever we go. Love and compassion; have deep compassion for the people. People are suffering much: mentally, physically, in every possible way. So you are the ones to bring that hope, that love, that kindness.

Do you want to do something beautiful for God? There is a person who needs you. This is your chance.

MOTHER TERESA

Our prayer for today:

Yes, Lord, we want to do something beautiful for You! People are hurting. Lead us to those who need Your love and hope.

October 27

. . . being knit together in love. . . .

Colossians 2:2

LOVE IS . . .

Love is not just looking at each other and saying, "You're wonderful." There are times when we are anything but wonderful . . .

Love is looking outward together in the same direction. It is linking our strength to pull a common load. It is pushing together towards the far horizons, hand in hand.

Love is knowing that when our strength falters, we can borrow the strength of someone who cares.

Love is a strange awareness that our sorrows will be shared and made lighter by sharing; that joys will be enriched and multiplied by the joy of another.

Love is knowing when someone else cares, that we are not alone in life.

Love is of God, for God is love. When we love, we touch the hem of the garment of God.

PATRICK SCANLON

Our prayer for today:

Oh, Lord Jesus, thank You for this gift of love that we have for each other. Today there are so many lonely people, looking for this special gift. Help us to reach out and bring them the news of how much You love them.

October 28

Let the peace of God rule in your hearts. . . .

Colossians 3:15

Someone once said, "Marriage is a mirage. When you look at it from a distance, it seems wonderful, but when you actually experience it, you are disillusioned."

For all too many couples, that is true. They manage to stick together, but no real love exists between them. As Billy Graham once said in a sermon, they live in a sort of armed truce.

The first institution established was marriage, and God intended it to be a beautiful thing. It is, in fact, a divine act that involves commitment and consecration.

In a conversion experience, our saying "I do" involves the yielding of our lives to Christ. Likewise, our saying "I do" in marriage should involve an unselfish surrendering to each other, with Christ at the center of both lives.

—B.B.

Our prayer for today:

Dear Lord, keep us from allowing our marriage to become mundane or boring. May we be constantly reminded that if we give You Your rightful place, that will never happen.

October 29

> But God showed his great love for us by sending Christ to die for us while we were still sinners.
>
> Romans 5:8 LB

In the Sermon on the Mount, Jesus said that if we love only the people that agree with us, what is so great about that? Even scoundrels and crooks love their fellow crooks. Jesus went on to say that genuine love is shown when God allows the sun to shine on the just and the unjust, and His rain falls on the good as well as the evil.

That may seem unjust to you, but let me assure you this concept is filled with mercy. And there will always be a tension between mercy and justice! If you are having difficulty forgiving someone because "what they did is just not right," let me encourage you to forgive as you have been forgiven.

ROBERT H. SCHULLER

Our prayer for today:

Lord, when we remember all that You have forgiven in our lives, we are humbled. Take from our hearts the judging attitudes that seem to come so easily to us. Forgive us, Lord Jesus, and fill us with Your love and compassion.

October 30

Love is very patient. . . .

1 Corinthians 13:4 LB

Patience is the quality which closes the gap between ourselves and others. It is a kind of heavenly courtesy which says, "I do not quite understand why you are as you are, but then I cannot understand myself; and since there is One who understands us both, let us extend to each other the patience He has had for each of us." Love without patience is not really love at all, but a shadowy vapor which will vanish at the first hot wind of reality, as the mists of night vanish when morning comes.

EILEEN GRUDER

Our prayer for today:

How often we need patience with each other, Lord. With fellow workers or friends, we find the grace to understand. At home, we become impatient with the one we should love the most. Take this fault from us, we pray, and give us patient, loving hearts.

October 31

. . . Lord, teach us to pray. . . .

Luke 11:1

. . . give God a chance. Take your problem, whatever it may be, to Him in prayer. Tell Him all about it—just as if He didn't know a thing. In the telling be absolutely honest and sincere. Hold nothing back.

Our minds are sometimes shocked when we permit our hearts to spill over, but it is good for our souls when we do.

If we would only have the courage to take a good look at our motives for doing certain things we might discover something about ourselves that would melt away our pride and soften our hearts so that God could do something with us and for us.

PETER MARSHALL

Our prayer for today:

Father, our culture often keeps us from breaking down and being completely honest. Strip away our masks, and help us to not be ashamed of tears or emotion. Take away our pride, and make us worthy to receive answers to our prayers.

NOVEMBER

November 1

> But if we walk in the light, as he is in the light, we have fellowship one with another, and the blood of Jesus Christ his Son cleanseth us from all sin.

> 1 John 1:7

Marriage is not a two-way relationship flowing between man and woman. It is a three-way relationship. As we walk in the Spirit, God gives us a love for each other which will flow spontaneously! A breakdown in our relationship as partners will inevitably entail a breakdown in our relationship with God. In fact, Bev and I have used a collapse between us as a signal that we were not walking in the Spirit. By confessing that sin to God, we opened our eyes to the problem.

TIM and BEV LAHAYE

Our prayer for today:

We ask ourselves today, "Are we really walking close to You, Father? Are there any barriers that have come between us and You?" Speak to our hearts, and make us willing to change those things that grieve You.

November 2

> . . . you are joint heirs of the grace of life. . . .

> 1 Peter 3:7 RSV

God delights in having a husband and wife serve him together. He blessed the joint ministry of Aquila and Priscilla, as he doubtless did that of Peter and his wife, and Jude and his.

There are three basic reasons for Christian marriage. The first two can be common to all marriages; namely for the mutual help given and received, and for the institution of family life. The third, however, is peculiar to a Christian couple, for they can receive God's grace together. This clearly shows the importance to God of such marriages. They provide for God a special avenue of bestowal of his grace upon the shared life and upon humanity. Marriage was instituted by God, not by man. Was it for this reason?

WATCHMAN NEE

Our prayer for today:

Almighty God, thank You for bringing us into this union. May our lives delight You, as we serve You together, confident that Your grace will lead us each day.

November 3

> Commit thy way unto the Lord, trust also in him; and he shall bring it to pass.

Psalms 37:5

The horror of Watergate brought Chuck Colson to the brink of disaster. It was then he met Jesus Christ.

Sitting by the fire one night after his release from prison, Chuck and his wife, Patty, experienced one of those special moments that come to married couples whose lives are dedicated to Christ. Looking into his eyes, Patty told Chuck she had been watching him for several months and knew he had made a decision about his life's work for the Lord. "Prison work is your life, isn't it?" asked Patty.

This burden had been on Chuck's heart, and now his wife, whom he knew would prefer to lead a quiet, private home life, had also been touched by Jesus Christ to surrender everything to Him. Chuck says, "Patty was picking up her own particular cross and would be at my side, whatever came." It was as equally important for Patty to be called, without any regrets, as it was for Chuck.

So often we cling to what we feel will bring us happiness, afraid to let go of our desires. It is when we surrender completely that we experience the deep, underlying joy that Jesus Christ wants to impart to us.

—J.W.B.

Our prayer for today:

Thank You, Lord Jesus, that You make clear to us Your will for our lives, if only we will listen. Together, as we surrender to You, we experience a unity of purpose and a joy in serving You.

November 4

> And since we know that he invariably gives his attention to our prayers, whatever they are, we can be quite sure that what we have asked for is already ours.
>
> 1 John 5:15 PHILLIPS

Many of us have reason to know that many times God answers prayer in a different way from what we expect. We have come to Him about some problem, difficulty, or obstacle, and asked Him to remove it, but He has not done that. Instead, He has increased our strength in order to enable us to overcome it. We have asked Him to take away temptation which we feel is too strong to bear, but still it besets us. Has God answered prayer? Indeed He has, for instead of removing it, He has given us purity of heart and victory over the temptation.

ALAN REDPATH

Our prayer for today:

Thank You, Lord, that occasionally You do not answer prayer. You see the whole, while we see only the immediate. We know that in whatever circumstances we find ourselves, You will give us strength to overcome.

November 5

> . . . Render therefore unto Caesar the things which are Caesar's; and unto God the things that are God's.

> Matthew 22:21

Let us listen to Christ saying, *"Render unto Caesar the things that are Caesar's"*—let duty and work have their place—"and unto God the things that are God's." Let the worship in the Spirit, the entire dependence and continued waiting upon God for the full experience of His presence and power every day, and the strength of Christ working in us, ever have the first place. The whole question is simply this, Is God to have the place, the love, the trust, the time for personal fellowship He claims, so that all our working shall be God working in us?

ANDREW MURRAY

Our prayer for today:

Almighty God, may we always give You first place in our lives. It is so easy for us to be guilty of allowing people and material possessions to come between us, Lord. May we take time to worship the One who has brought us together.

November 6

> For now we see in a mirror dimly. . . .

> 1 Corinthians 13:12 RSV

The most wonderful of all things in life, I believe, is the discovery of another human being with whom one's relationship has a glowing depth, beauty, and joy as the years increase. This inner progressiveness of love between two human beings is a most marvelous thing, it cannot be found by looking for it or by passionately wishing for it. It is a sort of Divine accident.

SIR HUGH WALPOLE

Our prayer for today:

Lord Jesus, thank You for the day we discovered each other. Your divine gift is one that grows as we love and respect each other through the years.

November 7

> . . . but in lowliness of mind let each esteem other better than themselves. Look not every man on his own things, but every man also on the things of others.
>
> Philippians 2:3, 4

Thoughtfulness is the beginning of great sanctity. If you learn this art of being thoughtful, you will become more and more Christ-like for His heart was meek and He always thought of others. Jesus went about doing good. Mary, His mother, did nothing else in Cana but thought of the needs of others and made their needs known to Jesus.

MOTHER TERESA

Our prayer for today:

Lord, often we are unthoughtful of other's needs. Teach us to be a couple that cares and reaches out to others—not to glorify ourselves, but You, Lord Jesus.

November 8

> Sorrow is better than laughter: for by the sadness of the countenance the heart is made better.

> Ecclesiastes 7:3

Sorrow in this world can become such a weight that many people go down under it, entirely discouraged. To others, sorrow is a challenge and they use it to lift them to higher planes, to greater sympathy and understanding. It forces many a person to look to Christ who "always causeth us to triumph in him."

HENRIETTA MEARS

Our prayer for today:

Dear Jesus, in times of sorrow we look to You, our Lord and Comforter. May these times draw us closer to You, so we may experience the wonder of Your loving consolation.

November 9

> The Lord is my shepherd. . . .

> Psalms 23:1

Not *was,* not *may be,* nor *will be.* "The Lord is my shepherd," *is* on Sunday, *is* on Monday, and *is* through every day of the week; *is* in January, *is* in December, and every month of the year; *is* at home, and *is* in China; *is* in peace, and, *is* in war; in abundance, and in penury.

J. HUDSON TAYLOR

Our prayer for today:

Thank You, Lord, that wherever we are, You are guiding us. This knowledge brings peace, as we are led by such a loving Shepherd, Lord Jesus.

November 10

> For none of us liveth to himself. . . .
>
> Romans 14:7

One characteristic of a Christian home is that our joy and our pain are shared with one another. When you share your joy with another person or another group of individuals, that joy actually spreads. It is infectious, spreading from one person to another, and they are able to be joyful with you. In Romans 12:15 we read that we are to "rejoice with those who rejoice" and to "weep with those who weep." In Galatians 6:2 we are told that we are to "bear one another's burdens," but how in the world are we to bear another's burdens unless that person is willing to share the burden with us?

H. NORMAN WRIGHT
and
REX JOHNSON

Our prayer for today:

Father, thank You for this life we share together. May we respect each other's feelings, so that neither of us will be reticent to tell the other of any burdens. Then, too, Lord, we will really be able to share each other's joys!

November 11

> Be kind to each other, be compassionate. Be as ready to forgive others as God for Christ's sake has forgiven you.
>
> Ephesians 4:32 PHILLIPS

Paul Tournier, the great Swiss Christian psychiatrist, feels so strongly about the need for understanding in the Christian marriage he says, "A husband and wife should become *preoccupied* with it—lost in it—engrossed to the fullest in learning what makes the other one tick, what the other likes, dislikes, fears, worries about, dreams of, believes in, and *why* he or she feels that way."

The Bible made the same recommendation many centuries ago. "Be kind to one another; be understanding. Be as ready to forgive others as God for Christ's sake has forgiven" (Ephesians 4:32, J.B. PHILLIPS). That's a text worth memorizing, or, better yet, worth placing in a conspicuous spot for all members of your family to see. For to know all is to understand. To understand all is to love. To love is to forgive.

JOHN ALLAN LAVENDER

Our prayer for today:

Lord Jesus, we would have the understanding love Paul spoke of. How we need it, to be to each other what You intended. Petty hurts and selfish desires often obstruct our being kind. Forgive us, Lord.

November 12

> If ye abide in me, and my words abide in you, ye shall ask what
> ye will, and it shall be done unto you.
>
> John 15:7

Telling God frankly what I have to say to him, and listening to what he has quite personally to say to me—this is the dialogue which makes me a person, a free and responsible being. It means being in fellowship with God, and that is faith. It is what the Bible calls "knowing God," "knowing his name"—that is to say his person, for the name is the symbol of the person. Even if it is only a fugitive moment, that moment is creative: the person awakes and emerges. It is as if the whole of the rest of the world becomes as nothing; this dialogue is all that matters. The personage I put on in ordinary life is no longer of any avail to me: God does not stop at the personage—he goes straight to the person.

PAUL TOURNIER

Our prayer for today:

Lord, You know our thoughts, our motives. We cannot hide from You. May our dialogue be honest, as we pour our hearts out to You.

November 13

> Since the Lord is directing our steps, why try to understand every-
> thing that happens along the way?

> Proverbs 20:24 LB

When the person you want to be is the same person God wants you to be, the possibilities for growing and becoming are almost limitless because you and God will be working in partnership to bring about the same end. You won't find a better partner to go through life with than the Lord Almighty. I saw a poster a couple of years ago at a youth retreat. The statement was unsigned but it said just what we are talking about:

"Freedom is not the right to live as we wish, it is the right to learn how we ought to live in order to fulfill all our potentialities."

DANIEL C. STEERE

Our prayer for today:

Lord, we would be a couple whose lives radiate what *You* desire. Use us to help alleviate the suffering in the world, we pray.

November 14

> For whosoever will save his life shall lose it. . . .

> Matthew 16:25

Loving others can be truly accomplished only when the focus of our minds and the object of our desires is another, when all of our activity results from concern for another and not from concern for ourselves. We have said that if a person truly loves in this way, he will be loved and he should accept the love of others. However the delusion to be avoided at all costs is to love in order to receive this return. I must, as Christ suggests, lose my life before I can gain it. I must find out that the only real receiving is in giving. I have to lose my life and I cannot lose it if I always have it clearly before my own mind.

JOHN POWELL

Our prayer for today:

Jesus, teach us Your selfless love. We would love each other in such a way that our loved one's welfare and happiness will be our true desire.

November 15

> . . . tribulation worketh patience; And patience, experience; and experience, hope; And hope maketh not ashamed. . . .
>
> Romans 5:3–5

God never promised to remove temptation from us, for even Christ was subject to it. The Bible says that "He was tested in all things, like as we, yet without sin." There is really no good reason why you should seek to escape, for such times of testing have beneficial effects. There is a sense of achievement and assurance that results from victory over temptation that cannot come to us otherwise. Temptation shows what people really are. It does not make us Christian or un-Christian. It does make the Christian stronger and causes him to discover resources of power. You can benefit from what might be tragedy, if you will only discover that in just such a time of temptation, Christ can become more real to you than ever, and His salvation will become more meaningful.

BILLY GRAHAM

Our prayer for today:

May we recognize when we are being tempted and claim the power that helps us resist—the name of Jesus Christ.

November 16

> And because ye are sons, God hath sent forth the Spirit of his Son into your hearts, crying, Abba, Father.
>
> Galatians 4:6

Tell God all that is in your heart, as one unloads one's heart to a dear friend. People who have no secrets from each other never want subjects of conversation; they do not weigh their words, because there is nothing to be kept back. Neither do they seek for something to say; they talk out of the abundance of their hearts, just what they think. Blessed are they who attain to such familiar, unreserved intercourse with God.

FRANÇOIS DE FÉNELON

Our prayer for today:

Father, You know our thoughts, our motives; there is nothing we can hide from You. May our prayers be filled with honesty and love for You.

November 17

Redeeming the time. . . .

Ephesians 5:16

Husbands *and* wives should constantly guard against the scourge of overcommitment. Even worthwhile and enjoyable activities become damaging when they consume the last ounce of energy or the remaining free moments in the day. Though it is rarely possible for a busy family, everyone needs to waste some time every now and then—to walk along kicking rocks and thinking pleasant thoughts.

You must resolve to slow your pace; *you* must learn to say "no" gracefully; *you* must resist the temptation to chase after more pleasures, more hobbies, more social entanglements; *you* must "hold the line" with the tenacity of a tackle for a professional football team blocking out the intruders and defending the home team. In essence, three questions should be asked about every new activity that presents itself: Is it worthy of our time? What will be eliminated if it is added? What will be its impact on our family life?

JAMES DOBSON

Our prayer for today:

Lord, we pray for discernment each day, to know the activities in which we should become involved. Especially help us to spend time with each other and with You, our Lord and Savior.

November 18

> . . . Holy Father, keep through thine own name those whom thou hast given me, that they may be one, as we are.
>
> John 17:11

God's plan for marriage—yours and mine—is that a couple achieve oneness. In other words, one man plus one woman should equal one great couple. That doesn't happen in most marriages. For many, one man plus one woman simply equals one man plus one woman. I believe that happens because for a marriage to add up to oneness, a third Person is needed. One man plus one woman plus God equals one great relationship.

When God is present, His love is present; and God-love enhances, purifies and beautifies the natural loves of a couple. I truly believe with Dwight Hervey Small that "a Christian marriage can never fail, but the people in that marriage can fail . . . So if the marriage of two Christians seems to fail, it is either that they were ignorant of God's purpose, or unwilling to commit themselves to it."

PAMELA HEIM

Our prayer for today:

Father, we pray that You will always be the head of our marriage and home. May we know Your will and live committed lives for Jesus' sake.

November 19

> He that is slow to anger is better than the mighty; and he that
> ruleth his spirit than he that taketh a city.

> Proverbs 16:32

. . . much of our anger is a very unbecoming expression of selfishness.
We are thinking about how we have been hurt, or somebody got what
we wanted. When it is all over, we are the ones who are hurt.

It has been said that the deafness of the great musician Beethoven
was caused by a sudden fit of anger. If that is true, think of the tragedy
here. The great musician could never hear even his own music.

Sometimes people say, "I get angry quickly, but I get over it." You
can say the same thing about a cyclone. It doesn't linger around very
long, but it does a lot of damage while it's there.

CHARLES L. ALLEN

Our prayer for today:

When we are angry, Lord, help us to express to each other, in a
Christlike way, how we feel. Heal the hurts, Lord Jesus, and forgive.

November 20

> A joyful heart makes a cheerful face, But when the heart is sad,
> the spirit is broken. . . . All the days of the afflicted are bad, But
> a cheerful heart has a continual feast.

> Proverbs 15:13, 15 NAS

A joyful heart is good medicine (the Hebrew says, ". . . causes good
healing . . .") *but a broken spirit dries up the bones* (Proverbs 17:22).
Honestly now . . . how's your sense of humor? Are the times in which
we live beginning to tell on you—your attitude, your face, your outlook? If you aren't sure, ask those who live under your roof, they'll
tell you! Solomon talks straight, too. He (under the Holy Spirit's direction) says that three things will occur in the lives of those who
have lost their capacity to enjoy life: (1) a broken spirit, (2) a lack of

inner healing, and (3) dried-up bones. What a barren portrait of the believer!

CHARLES R. SWINDOLL

Our prayer for today:

Create in our hearts Your continual joy, Lord, so that even when times are difficult, we will radiate the wonder of Your love.

November 21

> These things have I written unto you that believe on the name of the Son of God; that ye may know that ye have eternal life. . . .
>
> 1 John 5:13

Not long ago a radio announcer in Chicago took a survey in a train station. He asked about twenty-five or thirty people if they knew for sure that they were going to heaven. The result was interesting—a unanimous no. In fact, several became indignant and said: "Nobody can know such a thing as that!"

Contrast this with the statement by the great scientist, Sir Michael Faraday, discoverer of magnetism, who on his deathbed was asked: "What speculations do you have about life after death?"

"Speculations!" he replied in astonishment. "Why I have no speculations! I'm resting on certainties! I know whom I have believed, and am persuaded that He is able to keep that which I have committed unto Him against that day."

This certainty of heaven is not only the possession of the great and wise of the world, but also the poor and humble.

D. JAMES KENNEDY

Our prayer for today:

Lord Jesus, thank You for the assurance of eternal life. As we read and *believe* Your Word, we rejoice to think of all You have prepared for us, unworthy as we are.

November 22

> . . . in thy presence is fulness of joy. . . .

> Psalms 16:11

Happiness is not dependent on happenings, but on relationship in the happenings.

My father taught me this when I was just a child. He often told me of the early days of his marriage. He had opened a small jewelry store in a narrow house in the heart of the Jewish section of Amsterdam. Poor Mother! She had dreamed of a home with a little garden. She loved beautiful things and spacious views. "I love to see the sky," she often said. Instead, she found herself on a narrow street, in an old house—the kind with only a single room on each story—with worn-out furniture which they had inherited from Grandmother. Yet they were both happy, not because of the circumstances but because of the relationships in the circumstances.

CORRIE TEN BOOM

Our prayer for today:

Lord, we look at all You have provided for us—our love and our home. Thank You, Lord Jesus. Let us always remember, as Corrie's parents did, that "things" and circumstances do not bring happiness. It is the relationship that counts.

November 23

> When Jesus therefore saw her weeping, and the Jews also weeping which came with her, he groaned in spirit, and was troubled.

> John 11:33

Jesus Himself was open and vulnerable. He was sensitive to others' feelings. When He came upon Mary and Martha hurting because of Lazarus' death, He wept with them. The Jewish people thought He was weeping because of His love for Lazarus. But within that love Jesus was probably moved by compassion because of His sensitivity to the pain of the loss of Mary and Martha. When you let a family member venture into your world of feelings you then begin to develop true intimacy.

Apply this principle to your prayer life. Can you remember the last time when you "agonized" in prayer? When there was so much tremendous feeling behind it that you were almost crying out to the Lord? Unfortunately, it often takes a crisis for us to do this.

H. NORMAN WRIGHT and
REX JOHNSON

Our prayer for today:

Lord Jesus, we look at the enormity of Your compassion and see that ours is minute, in comparison. As we pray, may our hearts cry out to You for those we love and for the world.

November 24

What therefore God hath joined together, let not man put asunder.

Mark 10:9

What if Jesus decided to divorce His bride? That's just inconceivable, isn't it?

Then imagine the pain that God must feel when our marriage vows are broken asunder! Can you believe God to create *new* circumstances in a failing marriage? To come to the rescue with miraculous healing for the "one flesh" He put together? All of us know of some tragic breakup that has taken place or a union that's in trouble even now. Let's pray together against this threat to the body of Christ; let's commit every marriage we know into His keeping.

PAT BOONE

Our prayer for today:

Lord Jesus Christ, we remember our wedding day, when we vowed to love and to cherish each other until death would part us. Today, we vow again to love each other through You. We pray for all those married couples we know; may they be completely committed to You.

November 25

For as he thinketh in his heart, so is he. . . .

Proverbs 23:7

One of the basic factors for better homes is better attitudes. A family's attitude is more important than the family budget. Attitude can change the budget, but the budget seldom changes the attitude. Husband is an attitude, then provider; wife is an attitude, then mother; sex is an attitude, then pleasure. All deep and meaningful relationships in the home are founded on correct attitudes.

DON H. POLSTON

Our prayer for today:

Help us to examine our attitudes, Lord. May our home reflect a Christlike atmosphere, as each of us lives for You. Let our attitude be one of thankfulness to You, Lord Jesus.

November 26

Be still, and know that I am God. . . .

Psalms 46:10

Sometimes it seems that everybody wants something from God. I wonder what percentage of the prayers that reach heaven every day are asking for something. There is nothing wrong with that of course, but I wonder if God doesn't get "lonely" sometimes to talk to people who have nothing in mind but just being with Him, person to person. We all know how good it feels to talk with someone who is not trying to prove anything, who is relaxed about himself, and just enjoys being with you fully. Well, God must Himself be a million times more relaxed—and relaxing—to talk with. Certainly that ought to be part of our "praise" and "thankfulness," the experience of just being with God and experiencing Him as Himself.

CONSTANCE P. THARP

Our prayer for today:

Today, Lord, we want to say how much we love You! Our praise and thankfulness come from hearts that are grateful for the knowledge of Your faithfulness and goodness.

November 27

> Every good gift and every perfect gift is from above, and cometh down from the Father of lights. . . .
>
> James 1:17

Whatever brings two people joy and a sense of well-being is right for them . . . and when these are affirmed again and again as they are when the couple are together sexually, they are people deeply blessed. In poetic, symbolic language, Proverbs speak often of the pleasure and joy of lovemaking. . . . "Let your fountain be blessed, and *rejoice* in the wife of your youth, a lovely hind, a graceful doe. Let her affection fill you at all times with *delight,* be infatuated always with her love" (5:18, 19 RSV). "My beloved put his hand to the latch, and my heart was *thrilled* within me" (Song of Solomon 5:4 RSV, italics mine).

Rejoice . . . delight . . . thrill . . . words of pleasure and joy . . . words that put us in touch with ourselves as sexual beings and help to free us to enjoy our humanity *and* our spirituality. For part of our praise to God is in our emancipated celebration of sex, and in "guiltless gratitude" thanking him for his good gift.

COLLEEN and LOUIS EVANS, JR.

Our prayer for today:

Almighty God, your gift we receive with grateful hearts. Our times together are beautiful because we love through the joy of freedom in You.

November 28

> . . . Thou shalt love thy neighbour as thyself. . . .
>
> Mark 12:31

If you are going to be able to value others, you must first be able to see something of value in yourself. If you do not love (in the truest sense of the word) and value yourself, you will be unable to value others.

Some Christian writers have questioned whether self-love is biblical. Did Jesus really mean that we should love our neighbor as ourselves *as a command,* or was He merely saying in effect, "You already love yourself too much and you should therefore love your neighbor just as much"? In other words, is Jesus presupposing self-love—or is He commanding it? There is no doubt in my mind that Jesus is addressing Himself primarily to the error of misunderstanding the term *neighbor,* and that He presupposes self-love. Paul does the same in Ephesians 5:28 when he tells us to love our wives as our own bodies. In neither case is self-love condemned, however, and the difficulty we have with understanding it today is more a problem with what it means to *love* than anything else.

ARCHIBALD D. HART

Our prayer for today:

Father, we are "fearfully and wonderfully" made. Your creation— made in Your image. We know You love us. Help us to love ourselves in the right way, so we may reach out to our neighbors.

November 29

> Therefore being justified by faith, we have peace with God through our Lord Jesus Christ.
>
> Romans 5:1

We have obtained our introduction into grace from faith. By favor, God made grace available to us, and He made faith available as a key to grace.

It is as if you are going along in the midst of a terrible hailstorm.

Think of terrible, swirling, black clouds, strong gusts of wind, hail pelting down, injuring those who are in the midst of the storm.

Then suddenly, in the midst of all this darkness and devastation, there is a spot of light. You run for the light, and stand in it. In that light, there is no darkness, no fear, no confusion. There is blessing, happiness, and love. There is storm all around you, but you are safe, standing in the light.

This is symbolic, in a limited sense, of the grace that we stand in when we come to Jesus Christ and enter into the family of God. As His children, it is not our place to be in the maelstrom of the storm that swirls around us. We do not have to be buffeted around by all the torments that afflict the world.

PAT ROBERTSON

Our prayer for today:

Lord Jesus, thank You for the shelter You provide. Give us faith, we pray, to accept Your grace and love in times of trouble. Our eyes will be on You, our source of comfort and light.

November 30

> . . . we were so . . . crushed that we despaired of life itself. . . . but that was to make us rely not on ourselves but on the God who raises the dead.
>
> 2 Corinthians 1:8, 9 RSV

The pressure of hard places makes us value life. Every time our life is given back to us from such a trial, it is like a new beginning, and we learn better how much it is worth, and make more of it for God and man. The pressure helps us to understand the trials of others, and fits us to help and sympathize with them.

There is a shallow, superficial nature, that gets hold of a theory or a promise lightly, and talks very glibly about the distrust of those who shrink from every trial; but the man or woman who has suffered much never does this, but is very tender and gentle, and knows what suffering really means.

A. B. SIMPSON

Our prayer for today:

Dear Father, when we experience the "hard places," may our hearts and minds be so attuned to You that our heartaches will be turned into blessings for others. Our trials only teach us more of Your incredible grace and mercy. We praise You, Lord!

DECEMBER

December 1

Let love be your greatest aim. . . .

1 Corinthians 14:1 LB

Look around you at what you consider one of the best families you know in terms of functioning and meeting the needs of all its members. Remove all the kids and in-laws and grandparents and what you will probably find at the heart of it will be a husband and wife with a solid relationship. If they'll talk to you about it you will probably discover they have made a vocation of nurturing that relationship and have found the rewards worth it. The best preparation for parenting is a strong, growing relationship between husband and wife.

KENNETH CHAFIN

Our prayer for today:

Lord Jesus, may our love grow each day, through You, so that our family's spiritual and physical needs may be met.

December 2

If you love me, you will keep my commandments.

John 14:15 RSV

Love for God cannot divorce itself from delight to do His will, or else that love is little more than sentimentality. To suggest that because the New Testament stresses the spirit rather than the letter—and that this gives us liberty to void the letter—is unthinkable. Christian morality is not mere lawkeeping, but neither is it lawlessness (1 John 3:4). The danger of legalism must not weaken our love for and obedience to God's commands. The law of love is not a substitute for the moral law, but a summary and a fulfillment of it. Thus when the Scriptures speak again and again against fornication and adultery—against every manner of sexual sin—the obedient Christian will heed that word as his response of love to God. Biblically, love and law go together in perfect oneness.

DWIGHT HERVEY SMALL

Our prayer for today:

The closer we live to You, Lord Jesus, the easier it is to love You and keep Your commandments. May we always be worthy of Your love.

December 3

Thou shalt love the Lord thy God with all thy heart. . . .

Mark 12:30

When married people think only of happiness, they fall short of communicating the highest love of all. They in fact idolize each other, taking gratification in possessing and adoring their idol. Such devotion leads them away from God and from the Christian experience of love, since the two are dearer to each other than is God. The highest form of love liberates two people from idolatry, keeping them from dominating and possessing each other, and from demanding utter devotion as the price of love. Only God is worthy of utter devotion. So a couple are not to live entirely for each other, but must recognize that all love has its source in God. As loving husbands and wives, married partners are servants who mediate God's love, letting their love for each other serve a higher end.

DWIGHT HERVEY SMALL

Our prayer for today:

Father, let us keep our marriage vows sacred. May ours be a love that is devoid of self, utterly dedicated to You. Take our marriage and use it to serve Yourself, we pray.

December 4

> But without faith it is impossible to please him: for he that cometh
> to God must believe that he is, and that he is a rewarder of them
> that diligently seek him.
>
> Hebrews 11:6

Faith is not a human notion or a dream as some take it to be. Faith is a divine work in us, which changes us and causes us to be born anew from God (John 1:13). Faith "kills" the old Adam and makes us altogether different men, in heart, in spirit, in mind, in all our energies. It brings with it the Holy Spirit.

Oh, it is a living, creative, active, mighty thing, this faith!

MARTIN LUTHER

Our prayer for today:

Almighty God, fill us with Your Holy Spirit and create in us a faith that triumphs over our shortcomings. May our energy, our love, and our hearts be completely dedicated to You.

December 5

> Let him have all your worries and cares, for he is always thinking
> about you and watching everything that concerns you.
>
> 1 Peter 5:7 LB

God loves our loved ones more than we do. It is through prayer that we come to this grand realization. If we do little praying, we will find ourselves subconsciously believing that even though God loves so-and-so, He cannot possibly love him as much as we do! This is understandable, we reason to ourselves. After all, I'm related to that person. He isn't. She's my wife; he's my son or daughter or boyfriend—therefore, I am in a better position to really care and understand. Prayer suddenly becomes a sort of protective layer we must use to shield them from an angry, judgmental God, whom we believe is not very pleased with their life style.

Communication with God about people involves our spending enough time with Him to enable us to understand how He really feels about those we love. If we will only talk it out in prayer and listen to His answers, we will make a remarkable discovery. We will find out that we are not more merciful, loving and forgiving than God!

JILL BRISCOE

Our prayer for today:

Almighty God, thank You for lovingly caring for those we love. Teach us to *rest* in this knowledge. Forgive us for our needless fretting, and help us keep our finite hands off Your infinite work, Lord.

December 6

. . . I trust in thy word.

Psalms 119:42

Just in proportion to which we believe that God will do what He has said, so is our faith strong or weak. Faith has nothing to do with feelings, or with impressions, with improbabilities, or with outward appearances. If we desire to couple them with faith, then we are no longer resting on the Word of God because faith needs nothing of the kind. *Faith rests on the naked Word of God.* When we take Him at His Word, the heart is at peace.

GEORGE MUELLER

Our prayer for today:

Almighty God, we read Your Word and all Your promises, and our hearts find peace.

December 7

   . . . and the two shall be one.

Ephesians 5:31 LB

A Christian marriage has meaning and purpose even if God should give no children to the couple. The Bible speaks about marriage only in a very few places. So it is all the more striking that the same verse is quoted four times: "Therefore a man leaves his father and his mother and cleaves to his wife, and they become one flesh." (Genesis 2:24; Matthew 19:5, Mark 10:7; Ephesians 5:31). Notice how in this key verse, repeated four times, there is no word about children. According to the Bible, children are an added blessing of God. But they are not the only reason for marriage. The love of the two partners for each other, the becoming one person of man and wife before God, is a meaning of fulfillment of marriage in itself.

WALTER TROBISCH

Our prayer for today:

May we always be grateful for the gift of our marriage, Lord. Continue to make the love we have for each other grow each day. Let us never take the other for granted, Lord Jesus.

December 8

He must increase, but I must decrease.

John 3:30

The greatest burden we have to carry in life, the most difficult thing we have to manage, is self. Our own daily round of existence, our bodies and emotions, our private weaknesses and temptations—our inward concerns of every kind: these are the things that worry us more than anything else. These are the cares that most often rob us of our joy.

In laying down your burdens, therefore, the first one you must get rid of is yourself. You must hand over yourself and all your concerns into the care and keeping of your God, and *leave them there.* He made you; therefore He surely understands you and knows how to manage you, if you will only trust Him to do it.

HANNAH WHITALL SMITH
Paraphrased by
CATHERINE JACKSON

Our prayer for today:

Our Heavenly Father, how often we become overly concerned with ourselves, our bodily needs, our own satisfactions. We lay the burdens of self at Your feet. Help us to leave them there, so that we can be used for Your Kingdom. In Jesus' name.

December 9

> . . . God hath made me to laugh, so that all that hear will laugh with me.
>
> Genesis 21:6

I once heard a friend say, after the death of his wife, that what he missed the most were those intimate moments of shared laughter, the pet words and phrases meant just for the two of them. "There is no one to share them with, now."

The gift of a sense of humor is to be cherished—especially in marriage. How many times Bill and I have warded off a serious conflict by a few words that brought laughter, instead of anger or tears. There is an inscription in Chester Cathedral, in England, which reads:

> Give me a sense of humor, Lord;
> Give me the grace to see a joke,

to get some happiness from life,
and pass it on to other folk.

—J.W.B.

Our prayer for today:

Father, thank You for laughter, the safety valve that brings us back
to the reality of a situation and heals the misunderstanding.

December 10

If you will humble yourselves under the mighty hand of God, in
his good time he will lift you up.

1 Peter 5:6 LB

God knows what keys in the human soul to touch, in order to
draw out its sweetest and most perfect harmonies. They may be the
minor strains of sadness and sorrow; they may be the loftiest notes
of joy and gladness. God knows where the melodies of our nature
are, and what discipline will call them forth. Some with plaintive
song, must walk in the lowly values of life's weary way; others, in
loftier hymns, shall sing of nothing but joy, as they tread the mountain tops of life.

It does not matter how great the pressure is, it only matters where
the pressure lies; whether it comes between you and God, or whether
it presses you closer to His heart.

J. HUDSON TAYLOR

Our prayer for today:

Dear Heavenly Father, thank You for the writings of Your saints.
They speak to us, down through the years, of Your grace and faithfulness. May we learn to bear the demands of life positively, so that they
lead us closer to You.

December 11

... We saw certainly that the Lord was with thee. ...

Genesis 26:28

One day Malcolm Muggeridge watched Mother Teresa board a train in Calcutta. As he walked away, he said he felt as though he were leaving behind all the beauty and all the joy of the universe. "She has lived so closely with her Lord that the same enchantment clings about her that sent the crowds chasing after Him in Jerusalem and Galilee."

Lives that are completely yielded to our Savior cannot help but leave a touch of His love wherever they go. Even though Corrie ten Boom could not speak the language of many of the women in Ravensbruck concentration camp, they could sense Christ's love in her, and they were blessed. In her eighties, stricken by several strokes and unable to speak as she once did, Corrie still led people to her Lord. It was the glow of His presence in her life that spoke to the needy, longing heart of a woman who came to clean Corrie's home. Watching Corrie each day, she saw His love in her eyes and knew Corrie was praying for her. It was inevitable that she accept the Lord Jesus Christ.

Are our lives so transparent that when we are with others they sense His presence? In our daily walk with the Lord, can people—those in our home or outside—tell that we have been with the King of kings?

—J.W.B.

Our prayer for today:

Lord Jesus, may our lives be so completely surrendered to You that we will be able to reach out to others with the beauty of Your love.

December 12

God carefully watches the goings on of all mankind. ...

Job 34:21 LB

The lesson we learn from His silences and delays is that He is never before His time, or after. Because of His omniscience and omnipresence when the precise moment comes to act, He does so, decisively and beneficially, for He is a "very *present* help in trouble" (*see* Psalms 46:1). So, although He seems to tarry, we must wait, for He will surely come. "Our God shall come, and shall *not* keep silence . . ." (*see* Psalms 50:3). His seeming silence is not one of callous indifference or helpless weakness, but one which is a pledge of the utmost spiritual good for the sufferer. With a glorious end in view, the Lord does not spare from pain, but makes us perfect through the suffering endured.

HERBERT LOCKYER

Our prayer for today:

Teach us, Father, to wait on You. How many times we want to race ahead and see results—an end to suffering, an end to our problems. But Your timing is perfect. We rest in this indisputable knowledge.

December 13

> Then came Peter to him, and said, Lord, how oft shall my brother sin against me, and I forgive him? till seven times? Jesus saith unto him, I say not unto thee, Until seven times: but, Until seventy times seven.

Matthew 18:21, 22

Forgiveness does not depend on the cessation of offenses. While they were in the process of crucifying him, Jesus said, "Father, forgive them." One hopes the offense would cease, particularly that it should not continue repetitiously. Yet in the face of continuing offense, one can determine not to build up the barriers, but to keep open the avenues of communication to allow the flow of love, peace and good will.

Forgiveness does not depend on receiving compensation. It is reasonable, when possible, that recompense should be made for the offense. This may not be possible. Often all one can do is say, "I'm sorry. Please forgive me."

DOUGLAS ROBERTS

Our prayer for today:

Lord Jesus, help us not to build barriers, but let our lives flow with the grace of Your forgiveness and compassion.

December 14

> For God so loved the world, that he gave his only begotten Son. . . .
>
> John 3:16

Before our second son, David, was born, Joan and I read that it is a good idea to give any older child a present when a new baby comes home from the hospital, so that the older child would feel especially loved. Billy, our oldest, was then three. I splurged, buying him a fully automated toy garage. When we brought the baby home and presented Billy with his gift, he kept saying, "Wasn't it nice of him to bring me a present?" Both the baby and the toy garage were immediately accepted, with love.

When Jesus was born, God sent in Him a very special gift, to show us how much we are loved. God's gift of salvation began in a manger, ended up on a Cross, and was completed in His Resurrection.

As the Christmas season approaches, what can we offer Him? Christina Rossetti summed it up so simply, yet so profoundly:

> What can I give him,
> Poor as I am?
> If I were a shepherd,
> I would bring a lamb.
> If I were a wise man,
> I would do my part,
> Yet what I can I give him—
> Give my heart.

—B.B.

Our prayer for today:

Thank You, Father, for giving us the most magnificent gift that anyone could receive: the gift of love and redemption through Your Son. May our lives, our hearts, be a worthy gift for You.

December 15

Rejoice with them that do rejoice, and weep with them that weep.

Romans 12:15

To be sure, rejection is *painful.* I have often thought about the love of Jesus Christ in regard to rejection. Never has a human being loved so openly and authentically. And yet, crucified by men, forsaken by Father and Spirit, never has a person been so rejected!

The life of love does not excuse us from the pain of rejections. But the benefits far outweigh the pain. A single human relationship of sharing love is far greater than any pain which comes from rejection. Without a doubt, love is the greatest of all human experiences!

But love also demands the pain of inconvenience and personal identification. When you love another person, you are touched by her problems, questions, and hurts. Love celebrates when others celebrate and grieves when others grieve. Love shares *all*—even pain!

PAUL CEDAR

Our prayer for today:

Lord Jesus, may we be people who are worthy to be used by You to comfort and·rejoice with others. If rejection comes, we will remember the humiliation You bore for us, our Savior and our Lord.

December 16

Your attitude should be the same as that of Christ Jesus: Who, being in very nature God, did not consider equality with God something to be grasped, but made himself nothing, taking the very nature of a servant, being made in human likeness. And being found in appearance as a man, he humbled himself and became obedient to death—even death on a cross!

Philippians 2:5–8 NIV

What character Christ has!

Andrew Murray once mentioned that as water seeks to find the lowest level and fill it, so God seeks to fill us with the character of His Son when we are emptied, broken and low. When you think about it, that in itself is enough to give us real hope that even our most difficult sufferings are worth it.

JONI EARECKSON

Our prayer for today:

Lord Jesus, our sufferings—if we are completely surrendered to You —bring us hope. We thank You, that in the depths, we learn to be patient and filled with the glory of Your grace and love!

December 17

. . . He that believeth on me, the works that I do shall he do also; and greater works than these shall he do; because I go unto my Father.

John 14:12

Jesus Christ is the supreme human example of God-like courage. He was what He claimed to be, the very Son of God. He dared to make the claim. Have we this spirit of courage of the Lord Jesus Christ? Paul says, "I can do all things through Christ which strengtheneth me" (Philippians 4:13). Paul never feared because he knew the power of Jesus Christ (Romans 1:16,17).

HENRIETTA C. MEARS

Our prayer for today:

Lord Jesus, how we need Your courage to face the world. As we read of Paul, we, too, claim *power* in Your name. May our lives shine with Your bravery, Lord.

December 18

For he knoweth our frame. . . .

Psalms 103:14

Roy and I have those moments which every married man and woman have, when we are less Christian and less good than we should be. I would be less than honest if I said there had never been any squalls in my Christian walk or in our marriage. There have been tempests—but our house is built on the Rock, and it has stood firm through every squall and storm. We have grown together in our faith, and growing is sometimes a painful process. But with it comes—has come to us—a quiet, inner joy in knowing that by the grace of God we have learned to accept ourselves and each other as God's children and creation.

DALE EVANS ROGERS

Our prayer for today:

Thank You, Father, for Your acceptance of us, imperfect as we are. Teach us that same acceptance for each other.

December 19

As the hart panteth after the water brooks, so panteth my soul after thee, O God. My soul thirsteth for God, for the living God. . . .

Psalms 42:1,2

There are hungry hearts who will never realize their need because they do not know what it is they desire until one day they see the Lord

Jesus in you. It is that incarnate revelation of Jesus Christ in the life of a Christian which makes men and women thirst after God, for it crystallizes the thing that they have been seeking and cannot express. It meets the need of the heart which is burdened and lonely and troubled and does not know the answer. The moment they see a child of God who hallows the name of God, at that moment they see one who possesses what they need.

ALAN REDPATH

Our prayer for today:

Dear Lord, how often we fail You, as we meet those who need Your love. May we both live completely yielded lives that radiate Your concern and care.

December 20

> Who can find a virtuous woman? . . . The heart of her husband doth safely trust in her. . . . She will do him good and not evil all the days of her life.
>
> Proverbs 31:10–12

This Christmas I am giving . . .

To my husband—remembering how much he has had to put up with and for how long—I will give a frank, honest reappraisal of myself. I will ask myself, "If I were my husband, what sort of woman would I want to come home to?" (Every man being different, each of you will have to figure that one out for yourself.)

I will remember that happy marriages don't just happen. They are the result of good hard work. "A happy marriage," as the late Robert Quillen wrote, "is the union of two good forgivers."

Then I will take my Bible and reread those timeworn, ageless passages that speak of love and marriage and the responsibilities and privileges of wives. Sensible, delightful, down-to-earth passages, which if any woman would follow would make her husband the happiest, most contented man on earth.

RUTH BELL GRAHAM

Our prayer for today:

Our Father, how beautiful is the relationship of husband and wife, as *You* intended it! Let us give to each other, this Christmas, hearts that are grateful for the joy our love brings. Thank You for our happiness, Lord.

December 21

And Abraham said, My son, God will provide himself a lamb. . . .

Genesis 22:8

The most amazing thing about the Christmas story is its relevance. It is at home in every age and fits into every mood of life. It is not simply a lovely tale once told, but eternally contemporary. It is the voice crying out in every wilderness. It is as meaningful in our time as in that long-ago night when shepherds followed the light of the star to the manger of Bethlehem.

JOSEPH R. SIZOO

Whatever else be lost among the years,
Let us keep Christmas still a shining thing;
Whatever doubts assail us, or what fears,
Let us hold close one day, remembering
Its poignant meaning for the hearts of men.
Let us get back our childlike faith again.

GRACE NOLL CROWELL

Our prayer for today:

Lord, we look back to the wonder of Christmas in our childhood. Fill our hearts with that same wonder and joy. Let our faith in You, our Savior and Lord, shine so that others will learn of the meaning of Your birth.

December 22

> For unto us a child is born . . . and his name shall be called
> Wonderful, Counsellor, The mighty God, The everlasting Father,
> The Prince of Peace.
>
> Isaiah 9:6

He (Jesus) was the most balanced and perhaps the most beloved
being ever to enter the society of men. Though born amid most dis-
gusting surroundings, the member of a modest working family, He
bore Himself always with great dignity and assurance. Though He
enjoyed no special advantages as a child, either in education or em-
ployment, His entire philosophy and outlook on life were the highest standards of human conduct ever set before mankind. Though
He had no vast economic assets, political power or military might,
no other person ever made such an enormous impact on the world's
history. Because of Him millions of people across almost twenty
centuries of time have come into a life of decency and honor and
noble conduct.

W. PHILLIP KELLER

Our prayer for today:

Thank You, Almighty God, for Your gift to us that first Christmas.
Because of Jesus Christ, our hearts and lives are changed as we accept
His forgiveness and love.

December 23

> . . . Christ Jesus came into the world to save sinners. . . .
>
> 1 Timothy 1:15

Wouldn't it be wonderful if, in the midst of our joyous Christmas
festivities, there were some symbol or token which would remind us
that the Baby grew up? Long ago faithful men in northern Europe
brought into their churches and homes an appropriate reminder that
Jesus on His cross became the world's Saviour. That reminder was

branches from great holly trees. The sharp points on the evergreen leaves became for them symbols of the crown of thorns which was pressed upon the head of our Lord on the day of His crucifixion, and the bright red berries were representative of His blood which was shed for the remission of sin.

CHARLES L. ALLEN and
CHARLES L. WALLIS

Our prayer for today:

Lord Jesus, amid the decorations, so merry and bright, we thank You for the reminder of Your suffering on the Cross for us. Thank You, our beloved Savior.

December 24

> Surely he hath borne our griefs, and carried our sorrows: yet we did esteem him stricken, smitten of God, and afflicted. . . . and the Lord hath laid on him the iniquity of us all.
>
> Isaiah 53:4,6

Christmas is a time of joy, hope, peace, thanksgiving, and praise because the One whose birth we celebrate was marvelous in His Person and in His Work. He was God in the person of His Son, come to take away the sins of the world, to bear our griefs and carry our sorrows, to be wounded for our transgressions and bruised for our iniquities; for the sins of men He was to be stricken, and God in infinite love and compassion was to lay on His sinless body the iniquity of us all.

There is a new note of gladness to "Joy to the World" when we look beyond the Bethlehem fields to Calvary, and then on to the mount across the Kidron in the east—when, knowing that He has saved us from our sins, we hear the words of angels again: "This same Jesus . . . shall so come in like manner," and know that at that time we will meet Him in the glorious company of the redeemed.

L. NELSON BELL

Our prayer for today:

Our Lord, our hearts rejoice because of the love that came to the world that first Christmas!

December 25

> For because of our faith, he has brought us into this place of highest privilege where we now stand, and we confidently and joyfully look forward to actually becoming all that God has had in mind for us to be.
>
> Romans 5:2 LB

Jesus came to save his people from sin. That's the meaning of the name he was given. "You shall call his name Jesus, for he will save his people from their sins." He was Immanuel, God with us. He came not to establish the traditions of a new religion but to get to the inner heart of people's need. His life, message, death and resurrection were to reconcile us with God eternally. And that wondrous process for each of us begins in the healing of our inner selves. Our memories are liberated with forgiveness, our personalities are reformed around the person of Christ himself, our turbulent drives and needs are satisfied and reordered around his guidance and direction. The heart becomes his home. "The Father and I will make our home in you." The Christmas carol suddenly has meaning, "Where meek souls will receive him still, the dear Christ enters in." Then we can sing, "O come to us, abide with us, O Christ, Immanuel."

LLOYD JOHN OGILVIE

Our prayer for today:

Dear Jesus, because of Christmas, we know peace and joy. You came to forgive us, Lord, from all our sins. May our hearts always be meek as we remember what we were like without You.

December 26

> ... he will help us to be true to what we say, and not because we
> think we can do anything of lasting value by ourselves. Our only
> power and success comes from God.

> 2 Corinthians 3:4,5 LB

If you get a Bible and start to read about Jesus Christ, you might
be surprised to find in him the true pattern for your own life. It
happens to me many times. I get the feeling that I have goals that
can be accomplished by my own efforts. Then I read about Jesus
kneeling in prayer and realize that if Jesus—the Son of God, the
Real Man—needed to pray, how much more do I. I am not sufficient without God. Or sometimes as a preacher I get lost in words
and ideas and concepts. Then I look at Jesus, and what do I see?
Jesus was involved with *people.* He didn't just preach about leprosy;
he touched a leper. He didn't just lecture on hunger; he fed people
who had empty stomachs.

LEIGHTON FORD

Our prayer for today:

Lord Jesus, our sufficiency, our needs, can only be met in You. May
we look to You, our divine example and Savior.

December 27

> ... Give this man place. ...

> Luke 14:9

When our Lord was born into this world, no place was found for
him, either at the inn or in his Father's house, the Temple. There was
no room for him in Jerusalem. In his own city, Nazareth, they would
have pushed him over the brow of a hill. He was the "stone" of which
the builders said, "We cannot fit him into our building," and they
rejected him; but God made him the head of the corner. The place
that the world gave him was on a cross between two thieves; but the

Father exalted him to his own right hand and said, "Give this Man place."

ROY W. GUSTAFSON

Our prayer for today:

Lord, may there be no corner of our lives that You cannot enter. Our prayer is that You will always have first place, Lord Jesus.

December 28

> But he that doeth truth cometh to the light, that his deeds may be made manifest, that they are wrought in God.
>
> John 3:21

We walk as children of light when we insist upon transparent openness and honesty, no dark secrets, no duplicity, lies, or double-dealing. It was from my spiritual mentor, the Quaker Hannah Smith, that I learned the valuable lesson that hidden sin—no matter how carefully denied, glossed over and secreted away—will give Satan his beachhead and result in our inability to stand victoriously before the enemy or any of his cohorts. The emphasis here is on any accursed thing being tucked back in our lives, hidden out of sight. We may have almost forgotten about it, but Satan never forgets. For us, the result will be failure every time. This is the reason that Jesus had so much to say about the necessity of light and our coming to the light. When men's deeds are evil, they love darkness rather than light.

CATHERINE MARSHALL

Our prayer for today:

Father, make our lives transparent with Your light. If there is anything today that we are hiding from You or ourselves, we pray that Your Holy Spirit will reveal it.

December 29

> . . . ask, and ye shall receive. . . .

John 16:24

In what realm can one expect answers to prayer? In *all* realms. God cares about His people as individuals and has a gentle, tender love for us. We are told that some of His answers are that our "joy might be full" and "that the Father may be glorified in the Son." There is no doubt that the people of God are meant to have answers to prayer. There is no doubt that we are meant to pray, believing that He is able to answer. We should have a growing history—like a trail of footsteps behind us in an unbroken field of snow—which will bring to our minds that great reality which Jeremiah was reminded of as he looked back and spoke forth with great conviction: "Great is thy faithfulness. . . ."

EDITH SCHAEFFER

Our prayer for today:

Almighty and everlasting God, Your faithfulness overwhelms us as we look back and see the way You have answered our prayers. In Jesus' name, we praise You!

December 30

> . . . he went about doing good. . . .

Acts 10:38 RSV

Jesus never did harm to anybody. On the contrary, to everybody and in every circumstance he did positive good. We know what Jesus did. He saw, he felt, he acted. What about us? If we don't apply what we have to what we see, we are "closing our hearts" against our needy brother. And if we do that, John is provoked to ask the indignant question: "how does God's love abide in us?" It doesn't. It cannot, for divine love is service, not sentiment. So if his love is truly within us, it is bound to break out in positive action, in relating what we have to what we see. No wonder John ends with an appeal to us to be sure our love expressed itself not "in word or speech but in deed and in truth."

JOHN R. W. STOTT

Our prayer for today:

This day, we ask, Father, that Your compassion will flow through us, so that we will be able to be used to help anyone who is suffering.

December 31

For it is God which worketh in you both to will and to do of his good pleasure.

Philippians 2:13

If the old fairy-tale ending "They lived happily ever after" is taken to mean "They felt for the next fifty years exactly as they felt the day before they were married," then it says what probably never was nor ever could be true, and would be highly undesirable if it were. Who could bear to live in that excitement for even five years? What would become of your work, your appetite, your sleep, your friendships? But, of course, ceasing to be "in love" need not mean ceasing to love. Love in this second sense—love as distinct from "being in love" is not merely a feeling. It is a deep unity, maintained by the will and deliberately strengthened by habit; reinforced by (in Christian marriages) the grace which both parents ask, and receive, from God. They can have this love for each other even at those moments when they do not like each other; as you love yourself even when you do not like yourself. They can retain this love even when each would easily, if they allowed themselves, be "in love" with someone else. "Being in love" first moved them to promise fidelity: this quieter love enables them to keep the promise. It is on this love that the engine of marriage is run: being in love was the explosion that started it.

C. S. LEWIS

Our prayer for today:

Thank You, Lord, for the beauty of "quiet love"! As our marriage grows, this gift from You draws us even closer than when we were "in love."